W9-CXT-084

OPPOSING
VIEWPOINTS®
SERIES

School Safety

Other Books of Related Interest:

Opposing Viewpoints Series

Gun Violence

High School Alternative Programs

School Reform

Sexual Assault on Campus

Teachers and Ethics

At Issue Series

Bilingual Education

Cell Phones in Schools

How Valuable Is a College Degree?

Student Loans

Current Controversies Series

Bullying

College Admissions

Family Violence

Gangs

"Congress shall make
no law ... abridging
the freedom of speech,
or of the press."

First Amendment to the US Constitution

The basic foundation of our democracy is the First Amendment guarantee of freedom of expression. The Opposing Viewpoints series is dedicated to the concept of this basic freedom and the idea that it is more important to practice it than to enshrine it.

OPPOSING VIEWPOINTS® SERIES

School Safety

Noah Berlatsky, Book Editor

GREENHAVEN PRESS
A part of Gale, Cengage Learning

GALE
CENGAGE Learning·

Farmington Hills, Mich • San Francisco • New York • Waterville, Maine
Meriden, Conn • Mason, Ohio • Chicago

Judy Galens, *Manager, Frontlist Acquisitions*

For more information, contact:
Greenhaven Press
27500 Drake Rd.
Farmington Hills, MI 48331-3535
Or you can visit our Internet site at gale.cengage.com

For product information and technology assistance, contact us at

Gale Customer Support, 1-800-877-4253
For permission to use material from this text or product, submit all requests online at www.cengage.com/permissions

Further permissions questions can be emailed to permissionrequest@cengage.com

Articles in Greenhaven Press anthologies are often edited for length to meet page requirements. In addition, original titles of these works are changed to clearly present the main thesis and to explicitly indicate the author's opinion. Every effort is made to ensure that Greenhaven Press accurately reflects the original intent of the authors. Every effort has been made to trace the owners of copyrighted material.

Cover Image copyright © Nikola Solev/Shutterstock.com.

LIBRARY OF CONGRESS CATALOGING-IN-PUBLICATION DATA

School safety / Noah Berlatsky, Book Editor.
   pages cm. -- (Opposing viewpoints)
   Includes bibliographical references and index.
   ISBN 978-0-7377-7526-6 (hardcover) -- ISBN 978-0-7377-7527-3 (pbk.)
   1. Schools--United States--Safety measures 2. School violence--United States. 3. School violence--Prevention. 4. Schools--Security measures--United States. I. Berlatsky, Noah.
   LB2864.5.S35 2016
   363.11'9371--dc23
                            2015025546

Printed in the United States of America
   1 2 3 4 5   20 19 18 17 16

Contents

Why Consider Opposing Viewpoints?

> *"The only way in which a human being can make some approach to knowing the whole of a subject is by hearing what can be said about it by persons of every variety of opinion and studying all modes in which it can be looked at by every character of mind. No wise man ever acquired his wisdom in any mode but this."*
>
> *John Stuart Mill*

In our media-intensive culture it is not difficult to find differing opinions. Thousands of newspapers and magazines and dozens of radio and television talk shows resound with differing points of view. The difficulty lies in deciding which opinion to agree with and which "experts" seem the most credible. The more inundated we become with differing opinions and claims, the more essential it is to hone critical reading and thinking skills to evaluate these ideas. Opposing Viewpoints books address this problem directly by presenting stimulating debates that can be used to enhance and teach these skills. The varied opinions contained in each book examine many different aspects of a single issue. While examining these conveniently edited opposing views, readers can develop critical thinking skills such as the ability to compare and contrast authors' credibility, facts, argumentation styles, use of persuasive techniques, and other stylistic tools. In short, the Opposing Viewpoints Series is an ideal way to attain the higher-level thinking and reading skills so essential in a culture of diverse and contradictory opinions.

In addition to providing a tool for critical thinking, Opposing Viewpoints books challenge readers to question their own strongly held opinions and assumptions. Most people form their opinions on the basis of upbringing, peer pressure, and personal, cultural, or professional bias. By reading carefully balanced opposing views, readers must directly confront new ideas as well as the opinions of those with whom they disagree. This is not to argue simplistically that everyone who reads opposing views will—or should—change his or her opinion. Instead, the series enhances readers' understanding of their own views by encouraging confrontation with opposing ideas. Careful examination of others' views can lead to the readers' understanding of the logical inconsistencies in their own opinions, perspective on why they hold an opinion, and the consideration of the possibility that their opinion requires further evaluation.

Evaluating Other Opinions

To ensure that this type of examination occurs, Opposing Viewpoints books present all types of opinions. Prominent spokespeople on different sides of each issue as well as well-known professionals from many disciplines challenge the reader. An additional goal of the series is to provide a forum for other, less known, or even unpopular viewpoints. The opinion of an ordinary person who has had to make the decision to cut off life support from a terminally ill relative, for example, may be just as valuable and provide just as much insight as a medical ethicist's professional opinion. The editors have two additional purposes in including these less known views. One, the editors encourage readers to respect others' opinions—even when not enhanced by professional credibility. It is only by reading or listening to and objectively evaluating others' ideas that one can determine whether they are worthy of consideration. Two, the inclusion of such viewpoints encourages the important critical thinking skill of objectively evaluating an author's credentials and bias. This evaluation will illuminate an author's reasons for taking a particular stance on an issue and will aid in readers' evaluation of the author's ideas.

It is our hope that these books will give readers a deeper understanding of the issues debated and an appreciation of the complexity of even seemingly simple issues when good and honest people disagree. This awareness is particularly important in a democratic society such as ours in which people enter into public debate to determine the common good. Those with whom one disagrees should not be regarded as enemies but rather as people whose views deserve careful examination and may shed light on one's own.

Thomas Jefferson once said that "difference of opinion leads to inquiry, and inquiry to truth." Jefferson, a broadly educated man, argued that "if a nation expects to be ignorant and free . . . it expects what never was and never will be." As individuals and as a nation, it is imperative that we consider the opinions of others and examine them with skill and discernment. The Opposing Viewpoints series is intended to help readers achieve this goal.

David L. Bender and Bruno Leone,
Founders

Introduction

> "The United States is not the only country that has experienced violence inside its schools. On the same day as the Sandy Hook shooting, Min Yongjun wounded 23 children with a knife at Chenpeng Village Primary School. In 2010, China experienced five unrelated school attacks over the course of 50 days."
>
> —Andrew Freeman,
> "Just Enough or Too Extreme?
> School Safety Around the World,"
> TakePart, January 4, 2013

School safety is a major point of discussion in debates about US education. Students around the world, however, face safety issues as well. Some of the international school safety issues and solutions are similar to those in the United States. Others are quite different.

In China, one serious threat to student safety is the school bus. This is because school buses are not standardized or closely regulated. In November 2011, a minivan serving as a school bus hit a coal truck in Gansu province. The minivan had nine seats, but sixty-four people were riding in it. Nineteen students were killed and forty-three were injured. The public outcry led to an attempt to improve safety standards, but it has been difficult for Chinese companies to accommodate the demand for new, safer buses with capacity requirements and safety cages protecting the driver and passengers. As a result, foreign companies, especially American ones, have been trying to contract to provide buses to China. In the

United States, according to the National Highway Traffic Safety Administration, school buses are the safest form of transportation on the roads.

In Indonesia, school structures themselves are a source of danger. Indonesia is in a region that is prone to earthquakes. In 2009 an earthquake on the Indonesian island of Sumatra damaged 270,000 buildings, including 3,500 classrooms. An earthquake in 2013 in central Aceh damaged 514 schools. In order to improve the stability of schools in the event of future disasters, in 2010 the Indonesian government put together the One Million Safe Schools and Hospitals Campaign, which is dedicated to improving the safety of the nation's schools and hospitals. The country has made some progress on its goal of increasing school safety; in 2011–2012, 368,188 primary school classrooms were rehabilitated. However, the overall task is still daunting; it is estimated that 75 percent of Indonesia's 258,000 schools are in disaster-prone areas, and of these most were built in the 1980s, when earthquake proofing was not standard practice, according to Gogot Suharwoto in "Achievement of the Indonesian Safe School Implementation," a report prepared for the World Bank in December 2014.

Girls may face special dangers when attending school in many areas of the world. Girls are often subject to harassment and violence when they walk to school, a problem compounded in areas where students have to travel long distances from home. Schools themselves may be unsafe spaces as well; in 2010 in Zambia, for instance, there were two thousand cases of reported rape by teachers. Only 240 of the teachers were convicted, according to Jennifer Buffett in a 2012 article for CNN.

Girls may also be targeted by groups that believe that women should not be allowed to receive an education. In April 2014, for example, 276 female students were kidnapped from a high school in Chibok, Nigeria, by an Islamic terrorist organization known as Boko Haram. Boko Haram is opposed to modern education and particularly to the education of girls. The group often targets schools and kidnaps girls who it forces to act as servants and sometimes as sex slaves.

Hafsat Abiola-Costello and Bjarte Reve of the World Economic Forum's Young Global Leaders forum argued that to keep schoolchildren safe, Nigeria needs to concentrate on alleviating the pervasive poverty that has made Boko Haram attractive to some Nigerians. The focus on rescuing the Chibok kidnapping victims in particular, they say, has been misguided, since Boko Haram has been kidnapping and terrorizing other schools for some time. "What is required," say Abiola-Costello and Reve, "is an environment in which *all* abductions stop, along with all attacks on schools. However, where the majority of Boko Haram's potential recruits are not only unemployed but dirt poor, the battle to ensure safe children and schools must begin with the creation of broad economic opportunities for the destitute."

Some issues faced by American schools are also safety concerns in other parts of the world. For example, school shootings occur in other countries as well as in the United States. Germany experienced one of its worst school shootings in 2009, when Tim Kretschmer killed fifteen people in a school in Stuttgart. Just as school shootings do in the United States, the 2009 incident prompted a debate on Germany's gun control laws, which were already much tighter than those in America. Furthermore, just as in America, consensus was difficult to achieve, as gun club members resisted new legislation. Still, the German government did manage to create an electronic registry of firearms in an effort to increase security of handguns, according to a December 2012 article from Deutsche Welle.

Opposing Viewpoints: School Safety looks at issues concerning the safety of schools in chapters titled "Are Schools Safe?," "Can Better Gun Policy Make Schools Safer?," "Can Security Measures Make Schools Safer?," and "What Is the Relationship

Between Health Care Issues and Student Safety?" Different authors present opposing viewpoints on the question of whether schools are safe, and what can be done to make them safer.

OPPOSING
VIEWPOINTS®
SERIES

CHAPTER 1

Are Schools Safe?

Chapter Preface

Charter schools are often presented as the solution to the ills of the American public school system. Charter school proponents say the schools provide a better education than public schools. They also often argue that charter schools have fewer discipline problems, and are thus safer than traditional public schools.

Some research has supported the argument that charter schools are safer than public schools. For instance, Jon Christensen at the National Charter School Research Project found that during the 2003–2004 school year, "charter schools consistently reported significantly fewer issues with threats to persons or property and fewer behavioral problems than traditional public schools."

Similarly, Andrew Dunn, writing for the *Charlotte Observer*, compared incidents of violence in traditional public schools to charter schools in North Carolina for the 2012–2013 school year and found that there was significantly less violence at charter schools. Charter schools averaged 1.8 acts of violence per 1,000 students; traditional public schools had rates more in the 5 acts per 1,000 students all the way up to almost 10 per 1,000 students—almost ten times as many incidents of violence per 1,000 students as in charter schools. Dunn's research was not an academic study, and he notes that in some cases charter schools might be underreporting incidents of violence. Still, Dunn concluded, "I've heard parents say they opt for charters because they consider them safer and more orderly. These numbers seem to bolster their belief."

Others, however, have argued that charter schools are not safer than public schools. Kerry Fehr-Snyder writing for the *Arizona Republic* in 2013, for example, argued that charter schools in Arizona are not as prepared in terms of school security as their public school counterparts. Public schools in

Arizona have emergency response plans by law; charter schools are not required to prepare these plans. Many charter schools do have such plans, but others do not. Charter schools may be located in nontraditional locations, such as strip malls, without security cameras or protocols; they also may not have strict sign-in procedures.

Education activist Julie Woestehoff writing for the *Huffington Post* said charter schools can also threaten safety in other ways. In Chicago, Woestehoff pointed out, charter schools' locations require students to travel farther to school, often leaving their neighborhoods. This can mean that students have to cross gang lines, creating the potential for violence. New students coming into schools can also increase tensions. Charter schools, then, can contribute to a lack of stability that in turn can increase violence.

The following chapter examines whether schools are safe.

| "*Schools are not dangerous places. The perception that schools are dangerous is a misperception generated by a series of extreme, high-profile cases that are not representative of most schools.*"

Schools Are Safe Places

Dewey Cornell

Dewey Cornell is a forensic clinical psychologist and Bunker Professor of Education in the Curry School of Education at the University of Virginia. In the following viewpoint, Cornell argues that high schools are overwhelmingly safe places. Juvenile crime and violence have been declining for more than a decade, and the chance of a child being killed in a school shooting is small, he contends. Furthermore, myths about school and juvenile violence have led people to see schools as increasingly dangerous. These myths, Cornell concludes, are false.

As you read, consider the following questions:

1. Who was responsible for the school survey hoax, and what was their motive, according to the viewpoint?

2. What are the five myths that the viewpoint debunks?

3. What does Cornell say are common discipline problems at schools?

A widely publicized survey comparing public school problems in 1940 with modern school problems has been circulating for nearly twenty years, but the survey is a hoax invented for political purposes. The false survey of "top problems of public schools in 1940" listed items such as talking, chewing gum, and running in the halls. This list contrasted dramatically with an accompanying list of modern school problems that included drug abuse, pregnancy, suicide, assault, and other serious problems. In the 1980s and 90s, the two lists were widely cited by educational authorities and political pundits such as William Bennett, Rush Limbaugh, Carl Rowan, and George Will. The lists appeared in national newsmagazines such as *Time* and *Newsweek*, and newspapers such as the *New York Times* and *Wall Street Journal*; they were cited in numerous speeches and were aired on CBS News.

School Survey Hoax

A skeptical professor at Yale University, Barry O'Neill, investigated the origins of the lists and in the process collected over 250 different versions of the claimed surveys. Eventually, Professor O'Neill traced the surveys to T. [Thomas] Cullen Davis of Fort Worth, Texas. Mr. Davis was a wealthy oil businessman and fundamentalist Christian who in 1982 constructed the lists as part of an effort to attack public education. He shared the lists with some like-minded colleagues, who assisted in their dissemination. Asked how he arrived at the lists, Mr. Cullen told Professor O'Neill, "They weren't done from a scientific survey. How did I know what the offenses in the schools were in 1940? I was there. How do I know what they are now? I read the newspapers."

Although the lists were exposed as a hoax in 1994, they continue to be cited as factual. For example, at a 2001 school safety conference in a Midwestern state, an official from the U.S. Department of Education began her keynote address by presenting the same lists, unaware that they were fabricated. The point of this observation is that all of us are susceptible to misinformation about school crime and violence. Educators must be cautious about studies with bold or dramatic claims, and should demand credible evidence from firsthand sources.

According to Snopes.com, the mythical list appeared in a full-page ad in *USA Today*, placed by the American Family Association in July 2007.

Myths About Youth Violence and School Safety

The highly publicized school shootings of the 1990s generated nationwide concern about the safety of our schools. The news media focused national attention on little-known places such as Pearl, Mississippi; Paducah, Kentucky; and Jonesboro, Arkansas, where young boys opened fire on their classmates. In 1999, Columbine High School [in Colorado] became the best-known high school in America when two boys went on a shooting rampage that killed twelve students and a teacher before they killed themselves. Live television coverage of the Columbine tragedy began while students were still hiding in the school and police were attempting to find the shooters. In the following weeks, the American public was exposed to numerous images of bloody victims and interviews with traumatized, grief-stricken survivors.

There was a dramatic national response to the school shootings. Both the U.S. Senate and the House of Representatives held hearings on youth violence, the White House held a conference on school violence, and both the FBI [Federal Bureau of Investigation] and Secret Service conducted studies of school shootings. The U.S. Department of Education distributed "warning signs" guidebooks to schools giving advice on identifying potentially violent students and the U.S. surgeon general released a major report on youth violence. Less obvious, but even more important, local school authorities across the country adopted new security measures, implemented tougher zero-tolerance policies, and greatly expanded their use of school resource officers and school security officers.

Although the school shootings stimulated new attention to the problem of school safety and brought about many positive changes in relationships between schools and law enforcement agencies, public perceptions are easily skewed by media attention to a handful of extreme cases. The school shootings frightened the public and generated a widespread belief that there was an epidemic of violence in our schools. As the facts presented here demonstrate, this epidemic was a myth. School violence did not increase in the 1990s, it declined.

This pattern has been repeated after other high-profile shootings, such as the 2007 shootings at Virginia Tech [Virginia Polytechnic Institute and State University] and the 2012 shootings at Sandy Hook Elementary School in Newtown, Connecticut. The Newtown shootings prompted nearly 90% of school districts in the United States to upgrade their security at a cost of approximately 5 billion dollars. Although high-profile shootings in schools generate understandable concern, schools are objectively safe places with a very low rate of violent crime, including homicide. Approximately 1 percent of homicides of school-age children occur in schools. Statistically, the average school can expect a student to be murdered at school about once every 6,000 years.

The public may feel that school security is so important that the additional expenditures are necessary. However, multiple studies have found that the additional school security measures do not substantially increase school safety and on the contrary often make students feel less safe at school. When school funds are diverted to security, there is less funding available for teachers, mental health professionals, and prevention services. Educators should question whether they should sacrifice student support and prevention services in order to fund security measures of questionable value.

Consequently, it is important to guard against fear-based perceptions of school violence. Policy decisions about school safety must be based on objective information. School administrators and policy makers must maintain a rational and factual perspective on school safety. Here are five myths about youth violence and school safety that threaten to distort school safety policy and practices.

Myth 1. Juvenile Violence Is Increasing

Facts: According to FBI national arrest statistics, the arrest rate of juveniles for violent crime (murder, robbery, rape, and aggravated assault) peaked in 1994 and has declined each year since then. This rate is lower now than in any year since at least 1980. The most dramatic decline in juvenile violence is seen for homicides, the category with the most complete and reliable data. As shown [in the graphic], there were more than four times as many juveniles arrested for murder in 1993 than in 2013.

Myth 2. Juveniles Are More Violent than Adults

Facts: Juveniles account for just 11% of all violent crimes cleared by arrest. The peak years for violent crime occur in young adults.

Myth 3. School Violence Is Increasing

Facts: The rate of violent crimes in U.S. public schools has declined substantially since 1994. The serious violent crime rate (total number of aggravated assaults, robberies, and rapes per 100,000 students) in 2013 was less than a third what it was in 1994.

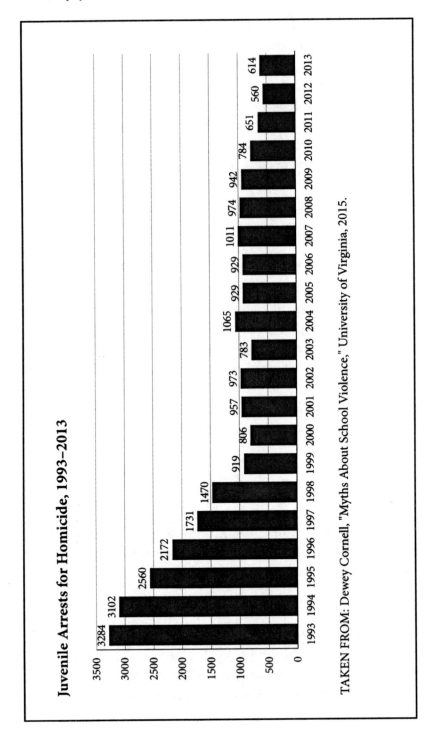

Juvenile Arrests for Homicide, 1993–2013

TAKEN FROM: Dewey Cornell, "Myths About School Violence," University of Virginia, 2015.

The drop in serious violent crime is not unique to schools. There has been a broader decline in serious violent crime in the United States since the mid-1990s.

Myth 4. School Homicides Are Increasing

Facts: Media attention to several school shootings resulted in a series of copycat crimes during the late 1990s, briefly interrupting an otherwise downward trend.

Myth 5. There Is a Realistic Possibility of a Student Being Murdered at Your School

The 2012 shooting massacre at Sandy Hook Elementary School in Newtown, Connecticut, stimulated tremendous fear that schools were dangerous places. Communities across the country diverted tax dollars to school security measures and armed guards. Fortunately, the tragedy in Newtown was an aberration. Homicides of students at school are rare events in comparison to the risk of homicide outside of schools. According to U.S. Department of Education data, there is an average of 21 homicides of students in the nation's 125,000 elementary and secondary schools each year. Simple division (125,000 divided by 21) reveals that the average school can expect a student homicide about once every 6,000 years.

A national study of school-associated homicides found that an average of more than two dozen school-age children were murdered every week in the United States, but only about 1% of those murders took place in schools.

Our study of homicide locations found that murders are statistically rare in schools compared to other locations. In a 37-state sample of 18,875 homicide incidents recorded in the Federal Bureau of Investigation's National Incident-Based Reporting System (NIBRS), only 49 incidents comprising less than .3 percent of the total took place in schools. The majority (52%) of homicides took place in residences and 30% took place in parking lots or roads.

Consider that restaurants have about ten times as many homicides as schools. What if there was massive media attention to every shooting in a restaurant with vivid accounts of the victims, survivors, and grieving family members? Would there be national concern about restaurant violence, a rush to fortify restaurant entrances, and a call from the National Rifle Association [of America] that restaurant servers should carry guns?

Gun violence is a serious problem in the United States, but this problem is less likely to occur in schools than almost any other location. According to the Centers for Disease Control and Prevention, there are approximately 84,258 nonfatal injuries and 32,351 deaths every year involving guns. These figures translate into about 319 shootings, including 88 deaths, every day in the United States. The gun homicide rate is far higher in the United States than other developed nations, and is at least seven times higher than rates in Australia, Canada, France, Germany, India, Italy, Japan, South Korea, Spain, Sweden, the United Kingdom, and many others.

How Dangerous Are Our Schools?

Schools are not dangerous places. The perception that schools are dangerous is a misperception generated by a series of extreme, high-profile cases that are not representative of most schools. In fact, very few serious violent crimes take place at school. From the standpoint of violent crime, students are safer at school than at home. Moreover, schools have become even safer during the past decade, such that the serious violent crime rate at school is less than half what it was in 1994.

Although there are relatively few serious violent crimes at school, there are many less serious crimes and there are numerous discipline problems—primarily disorderly conduct and fights that do not result in injuries—that demand attention. Bullying, teasing, and harassment are common problems that deserve attention in every school, too.

Schools are relatively safe, but they are not crime free and we have an obligation to keep them as safe as possible. To keep schools safe, it is important to recognize what kinds of crimes are likely or unlikely to occur, and to base decisions on facts rather than fears.

> *"Our public education system has be-*
> *come increasingly controlled by federal-*
> *level bureaucrats and politicians. It's a*
> *socialist system and like all socialist*
> *systems, destructive."*

Public Schools Are Fundamentally Unsafe

Rick David

Rick David is a writer at the ClashDaily website. In the follow-
ing viewpoint, David argues that public schools are innately vio-
lent and harmful to students. This is not just because of school
violence. For David, dangerous includes a curriculum that fo-
cuses on sex and sexuality, as well as the increasing amount of
data the federal government has access to about students and
their families. David says the school system is socialist and cor-
rupt, and he encourages parents to support moving students to
charter and private schools.

As you read, consider the following questions:

1. When does David claim sex education begins in schools,
   and into which subject areas does he say it is woven?

2. Why does David criticize the textbook *Your Health Today?*

3. What is the Youth Risk Behavior Survey, and why is David concerned about it?

Millions of schoolchildren are heading back to school. For too many parents, it's a relief. These days it often takes two working parents to support a family. School serves as a welcome babysitter. But most parents probably are not aware of how unsafe their child's school may be, and I'm not just referring to the dangers that they encounter from other students such as bullying and drugs. They also have to face threats from the public system and some teachers.

Dismantle Public Education

I've written here [at ClashDaily] frequently about the need to dismantle the public education monopoly. The socialist-style public system is costing taxpayers more every year and with diminishing returns. Continuing on this path is insanity. I have focused my concerns on the social/political indoctrination that students encounter, such as global warming hysteria, social justice/income redistribution socialism along with an anti-American bias. Liberal-minded parents may not agree with these concerns. But, there are other dangers facing public school students that I think would concern the vast majority of parents. The ever expanding emphasis on sex education and the nature of the curriculum should concern most parents. Sex education now begins as early as kindergarten. That's enough of a shock for most parents. Dr. Rich Swier and Dr. Duke Pesta have researched how the sex ed curriculum is now woven into every subject area. In math? Yes.

This interweaving makes it practically impossible for parents to opt out. There are widespread reports that the curriculum is increasingly more supportive of homosexuality as a "normal" alternative lifestyle and that significant time is spent convincing the kids of this. The curriculum is value free. There are no right and wrong behaviors taught. All forms of sexual behavior are taught as equally valid. Much of the curriculum sounds like it was written by Planned Parenthood [Federation of America, a reproductive services nonprofit organization]. That's not surprising given the close relationship between Planned Parenthood and the Democrats who control the U.S. Department of Education.

Pornography and the Classroom

Some parents find the curriculum to be pornographic in nature. Parents in Fremont, CA, have signed petitions threatening legal action over a ninth-grade health textbook featuring oral sex, vibrators and bondage. The textbook is called *Your Health Today*. Eighth graders at Woodland Park Middle School in San Marcos, California, were asked to stand under signs that said how far they would be willing to go sexually. The signs said, "smiled at, hugged, kissed, above the waist, below the waist, and all the way." A Bellingham High School drama teacher had to issue an apology after her awards ceremony devolved into an evening of profanity about a priest having sex with kids. A Gilford, NH, parent was arrested at a school board meeting for complaining about a pornographic book his ninth-grade daughter was exposed to. The book, *Nineteen Minutes*, by Jodi Picoult includes erotic sexual scenes.

Vulnerable Data

The federal bureaucrats have their hands in your school. The CDC [Centers for Disease Control and Prevention] sends out a Youth Risk Behavior Survey to all public schools that is given to children even in elementary school. The survey asks children about their personal sexual behavior. Most parents are not even made aware that the survey has been administered to their children. Now, Common Core [referring to the Common Core State Standards Initiative] has introduced data mining of student performance and attitudes by private contractors. Even the liberal *Politico* reports that, "The goal is to identify potential problems early and to help kids surmount them. But the data revolution has also put heaps of intimate information about schoolchildren in the hands of private companies—where it is highly vulnerable to being shared, sold or mined for profit." In 2010, the National Center for Education Statistics released a technical brief detailing that certain "sensitive information" could be extracted including political affiliations or beliefs of the student or parent, mental and psychological problems of the student or the student's family, religious practices and of course, sex behavior or attitudes.

Accompanying the ever increasing emphasis on sex, there has been an explosion of teacher sex assaults on students. Drive West Communications has tracked 416 cases across the country just since January of this year [2014]. Reports of such cases abound. KHOU-TV reported that a teacher gave a lap dance to a 15-year-old boy at Stovall Middle School. A Connecticut high school English teacher faced multiple criminal charges after she allegedly threatened to fail a student if he didn't have sex with her. An art teacher in Camden, NJ, asked boys to bring semen-stained tissues to school so he could make art projects with them.

Unions Protect Wrongdoers

What is frustrating in many such cases is an inability to or great delay in terminating such predators due to tenure protection afforded through union contracts. Fox News reported on the dirty dozen teachers protected by unions. One of these, a band director at O'Fallon Township High School in Illinois was having a sexual relationship with a 17-year-old female student. Instead of being fired, the teacher was able to resign, and the relationship was kept out of his file so he could obtain another teaching job. In 2010 he was convicted of molesting another female student and sentenced to six years in prison.

Of course, such cases may be rare. The majority of teachers are dedicated, hardworking and morally upright people. But, they are working in a corrupt system. Bureaucratic rules and union contracts protect bad teachers. And even good teachers have little control over the curriculum.

Our public education system has become increasingly controlled by federal-level bureaucrats and politicians. It's a socialist system and like all socialist systems, it is destructive. A private system would not only offer parents more choice and greater control, it would do the same for teachers.

My advice to parents is to abandon the system. It will collapse and force reform. Partner with groups like the American Legislative Exchange Council and StudentsFirst that advocate for vouchers and charter schools.

"It's estimated that 1 in 3 students will be bullied this year. *That is to say an estimated 18 million children will be subject to bullying."*

Bullying Means Schools Are Not Safe

Kristina Chew

Kristina Chew teaches and writes about ancient Greek and Latin; she is online advocacy and marketing manager at Care2. In the following viewpoint, Chew reports that one in three students is bullied, and she suggests that bullying is a pervasive problem in public schools. She points in particular to bullying of students with disabilities. Studies differ, she says, on whether students with disabilities are bullied at higher rates, but she notes that they can be especially vulnerable, not just to bullying from other students but to sexual abuse from caregivers. Chew concludes that schools are right to be focusing more attention on the dangers of bullying.

As you read, consider the following questions:

1. What are two factors that Chew says have been identified as hampering efforts to stop bullying?

2. What explanation does Chew suggest for the fact that bullies and victims in special education seem to do better overall than those in the general student population?

3. What special education challenges does Chew say that her own son faces?

August is half over: That means that school is starting soon for children across the nation.

But just how safe are our nation's public schools?

1 in 3 Students Will Be the Target of Bullying

I'm not talking about schools having metal detectors and police at their entranceways (though such have become the norm at more than a few schools I've been in). I'm talking about students bullying other students. On *EdWeek's [Education Week's] District Dossier* blog, Dakarai Aarons writes that, according to federal statistics, it's estimated that *1 in 3 students will be bullied this year.* That is to say, an estimated 18 million children will be subjected to bullying.

1 out of 3 students will be the target of bullying?

What can we do?

The federal government's first anti-bullying summit was held last week [in August 2010]. At the summit, some factors that have been hampering efforts to stop bullying were identified. These include

- a lack of consensus about what actually constitutes bullying, and

- a lack of knowledge about bullying and its potential effects on a child's health among pediatricians.

Some school officials are trying to combat bullying by saying that eliminating bullying is not simply an 'add-on' but fundamental to a change in school climate.

Bullying: Common and Dangerous

Customarily tolerated in Western society, bullying was not acknowledged or was considered a "normal" childhood experience, one perhaps with a positive outcome through character formation. . . . There is growing recognition that bullying is a public health issue that must be addressed.

Dan Olweus is regarded as the first to conduct research on bullying among children and youth, after the suicides of three boys in 1982 that were associated with bullying victimization. Olweus developed and evaluated an anti-bullying program . . . that targeted various levels of the system: the whole school, the classroom, and individual students. There has since been a veritable explosion around the world of research and programs and evaluations in efforts to understand and address bullying. Yet it has taken extreme cases in which bullying appeared to be a factor for this phenomenon to stop hovering and to truly enter the public consciousness. For example, analysis of the April 1999 Columbine tragedy [referring to the school shooting at Columbine High School in Colorado] revealed that one of the multiple factors that may have contributed to the killing rampage by Eric Harris and Dylan Klebold was their chronic victimization by popular school athletes. The horrific violence that occurred at Columbine represents extreme violence, which clearly does not occur in the majority of schools. Some students, teachers, and parents depicted the school as one in which bullying was tolerated, a not uncommon situation, especially when perpetrated by high-status groups such as "jocks."

Faye Mishna, Bullying: A Guide to Research, Intervention, and Prevention. *New York: Oxford University Press, 2012.*

I think this is an important shift in perspective to consider. Bullying doesn't only affect individual students. It can infect—infest—the climate of a school and the community that administrators, teachers, staff, and students and their parents seek to build. School officials need to work to make their schools safe for everybody.

Students with Disabilities at a Higher Risk of Being Victimized

Studies have shown that students with disabilities are at a higher risk of being victimized than 'typical' students. One recent study does, though, suggest that the rate at which students with disabilities and other students are bullied is the same. According to the *Child Psychology Research Blog*'s review of this same study, "both bullies and victims in special education seem to perform better over time than bullies and victims in regular education." This result may be due to the "effectiveness of the special education program," with children in special ed programs receiving "more targeted interventions that help them modulate the harmful effects of bullying."

Perhaps school officials might take a look at what sorts of interventions special ed students are receiving, that help "modulate" those "harmful effects of bullying."

Still, it is the case that students with disabilities are victimized and not only by other students. At *EdWeek's On Special Education* blog, Christina Samuels writes about a survey that is focusing on students with disabilities who have been sexually abused at school:

> In 2007, the U.S. Department of Justice released a report about crimes against people with disabilities in general. The report did not focus specifically on students, sex crimes, or crimes occurring in a school setting.
>
> However, the Justice Department did note that 12- to 19-year-olds with disabilities experienced violence at nearly

twice the rate of youths the same age without disabilities. People with cognitive disabilities had a higher rate of victimization than people of any other disability category. And more than half the violent crimes against people with disabilities were against those with multiple disabilities.

According to one study, "49 percent of people with intellectual disabilities will experience 10 or more sexually abusive incidents."

Again, these figures do not specifically apply to a school setting. But as the Hofstra University doctoral candidate Mary Lou Bensy, who is conducting the survey, says, students with disabilities are "'dependent on people who provide very personal support services,'" including toileting and other aspects of personal hygiene and self-care. Certainly skills such as washing hands and face, using the restroom, etc. are among the goals on the individualized education plans (IEPs) of many students with disabilities (my son included).

It should also be kept in mind that many students with disabilities (for instance, my own son, who is minimally verbal) may have difficulties communicating, and, therefore, may well not be at all able to report something like abuse.

So bravo to school officials for making bullying and the overall school climate a priority in the upcoming school year. But please, please, don't forget that special ed students are, sadly, likely to be victimized and even abused.

Special ed students are very, very much a part of a school community. And what kind of a community is a school in which some members do not feel safe?

"Studies tracking school violence and bullying since the early 1990s through 2010 show declines of between 25% and 75%."

Bullying in Schools Is Declining

David Finkelhor

David Finkelhor is the director of Crimes Against Children Research Center as well as a professor of sociology at the University of New Hampshire. In the following viewpoint, Finkelhor argues that bullying in schools has been declining since the 1990s. The reasons for this decline are not clear, but he speculates that it may be tied to changes in school policy, or in the wider availability of medications for mental illness. Finkelhor concludes that bullying rates are still too high, but the long-term decline should be acknowledged as a sign of hope.

As you read, consider the following questions:

1. According to the viewpoint, what does the National Crime Victimization Survey show about rates of theft in schools?

2. Have cyberbullying rates risen or fallen, according to the Youth Internet Safety Survey?

3. What implications does the decline have for evaluating anti-bullying programs, according to Finkelhor?

Highly publicized cases of bullying in recent years and new attention to the problem in schools have created the impression among some observers that the problem has been on the rise. But at the same time, crime and violence, including youth violence, have been decreasing overall in the US. Is this true for bullying and peer victimization?

In this [viewpoint], we will summarize the trends, from youth surveys that have tracked bullying specifically, and also those that have tracked closely related phenomena such as school assaults, school thefts, school fighting and school hate speech.

The surveys that reflect change over the longest time periods, going back to the early 1990s, consistently show declines in bullying and peer victimization, some of it remarkably large. The more recent trends, since 2007, show some declines, but less consistently.

National Crime Victimization Survey

The annual National Crime Victimization Survey (NCVS) shows that between 1992 and 2010 for youth 12–18 school-related violent victimizations declined 74% and school-related thefts declined 82%. The declines were fairly linear over this period and included a drop of 50% in school-related violence and 45% in theft in the most recent period from 2007 to 2010.

These declines in the overall NCVS were roughly confirmed by the specific school crime supplement of the NCVS conducted among 12–18-year-old youth at less frequent intervals. The school crime supplement showed a decline from 1995 to 2009 of 53% in violent school victimization and 61%

in school theft. The large decreases were across the board, affecting youth of both genders, all races and in urban, suburban and rural settings. They included small declines from 2007 to 2009 (12% for violent victimization).

The school crime supplement also asked about being the target of hate-related words at school. The trend showed a decline of 29% from 2001 to 2009. There were declines for whites and blacks but not Hispanics.

Finally, the NCVS school supplement began to ask a specific question about bullying in 2005 that was repeated in 2007 and 2009. The rate rose from 2005 to 2007 and then declined from 2007 to 2009 (from 28% to 32% and back to 28%).

Other Surveys

The Youth Risk Behavior Survey (YRBS) also has conducted large national student surveys (9th–12th graders) going back to the early 1990s. Between 1991 and 2011, the survey documented declines in youth physical fighting (down 23%) and in fighting on school property (down 26%). In the more recent time period 2007 to 2011, changes were slight in both: physical fighting (down 7%) and fighting on school property (down 3%).

The national YRBS began reporting specifically about bullying on school property in 2009 and found no difference between 2009 and 2011. However, in the YRBS survey conducted in Massachusetts a bullying question has been asked since 2003 and the rate there has declined 22% from then until 2011.

As part of an international project on the health of children ages 11, 13 and 15, representative national samples were surveyed on multiple occasions in 27 countries including the US. A question using the specific term "bullying" along with a definition was asked to inquire about victimization and perpetration. The longest span in the US compared 1997–8 with

2005–6 and broke down trends by gender. For boys, perpetration dropped 15.5% (occasional bullying) and 37.4% (chronic bullying) and victimization dropped 24.7% (occasional) and 27.0% (chronic). For girls, the declines were less dramatic, with perpetration down 4.1% (occasional) and 16.7% (chronic), and victimization down 0.7% (occasional) and 3.6% (chronic).

Another state, Minnesota, has a long-standing student survey that asked 6th, 9th and 12th graders every 3 years about "pushing, grabbing and shoving" on school property. The 6th graders, who had the highest rates overall, had a 19% decline from 1995 to 2010 in what was a linear trend over time. The 9th graders had an 18% decline mostly concentrated between 2001 and 2010. The 12th graders had very little overall decline and most of it wasn't until the period from 2007 to 2010.

The National Survey of Children's Exposure to Violence (NatSCEV) gathered information about victimizations of representative samples of children in 2006, 2009 and 2011. Between 2006 and 2009 it found a decline in physical harassment by peers but no decline in psychological harassment. From 2009 to 2011, there was no change.

Because of concern that aggressive behavior and bullying have transferred to electronic media, surveys have begun to assess this problem as well. The Youth Internet Safety Survey (YISS) asked a representative sample of US Internet-using youth about experiences of being harassed online. Rates increased from 6% in 2000 to 9% in 2005 to 11% in 2010, an increase of 83% over the decade.

[K.] Rigby & [P.K.] Smith reviewed trend information for bullying on the international level and concluded that most of the data pointed toward declines. "All nine of the data sets noted . . . showed some decrease in reported victimization, although for Norway there was evidence of a recent resurgence. In the international data set for boys and girls combined, 19 of the 27 reported cases showed a significant decrease in occasional victimization and 21 in chronic victimization. From this it appears that the prevalence of bullying among young people is generally decreasing."

Bullying Is Declining

Four US national data sets show substantial declines in face-to-face bullying and peer-related victimizations at school from the 1990s to recent years. Some of these are quite large. In general, the declines are broad across demographic groups. One study reports less decline in bullying for girls, but other indicators do not replicate this gender difference. Being the target of hate words may not have declined for Hispanics.

The trends for more recent years, beginning in 2006 or 2007, are fairly consistent but less dramatic. The NCVS violence measures since 2007 showed a large continuing decline. The NCVS school supplement and YRBS showed declines, including a small decline in a specific bullying question from 2007 to 2009 (although it rose from 2005 to 2007). NatSCEV found a decline for physical, but not psychological bullying.

On the other hand, Internet harassment appears to have increased in the 2000s. Could peer victimization have simply been displaced from the school to the electronic environment? Two factors argue against a simple displacement model. First, the declines in peer victimization date from the early 1990s, some years before the social media and mobile device revolution gained its dominion among youth in the early 2000s. Second, the main declines documented in the surveys are for physical assaults and property crimes that do not transfer to the electronic environment. Rather than a displacement, the increase in online harassment is probably best seen simply as growth in the usage of electronic media for all kinds of socialization including its negative forms. The strong overall conclusion from the available data is that there have been fairly substantial declines in face-to-face bullying and peer victim-

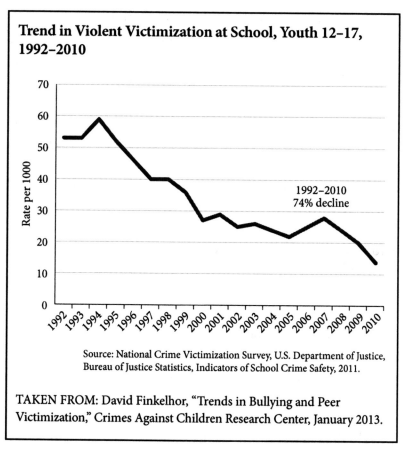

Trend in Violent Victimization at School, Youth 12–17, 1992–2010

1992–2010
74% decline

Source: National Crime Victimization Survey, U.S. Department of Justice, Bureau of Justice Statistics, Indicators of School Crime Safety, 2011.

TAKEN FROM: David Finkelhor, "Trends in Bullying and Peer Victimization," Crimes Against Children Research Center, January 2013.

ization in school since the 1990s with indications that the declines have continued in recent years.

Explanations and Implications

What are the likely explanations of these trends? Although the intensity of attention to bullying has risen in very recent years, the issue of violence and crime in school has been a problem of long-standing interest to authorities in education and law enforcement. One of the main innovations in school safety programs was the school resource officer (SRO) program, which delegates police to work in schools and try to develop and promote violence and crime reduction programs. The SRO grew out of community-oriented police (COPS) funding in the mid to late 1990s. One estimate was that, "in 1999, 30 percent of local police departments, employing 62 percent of all officers, had about 9,100 full-time school resource officers assigned to schools."

At the same time, curriculum developers created a wide array of bullying and violence prevention programs for school-age children, some of which have proven effective in scientific evaluation. Surveys suggest that considerable portions of school-age populations in the US have been exposed to such programs. Given this mobilization since the 1990s, it may be that efforts of school personnel and school curricula on preventing violence and crime have had some role in reducing its prevalence.

At the same time that bullying apparently has been declining, other indicators of crime and youth deviance have also been improving. Homicide and suicide rates among a broad age spectrum of the population have been decreasing. Most kinds of crime involving offenders at most ages have also gone down. This may reflect active crime prevention efforts at many levels, but it is also possibly related to some general social changes that might affect crime, violence and deviance more generally. There are several possible candidates. One has been the advent of electronic media and mobile communication. These technologies may have dampened crime and bullying by providing more ways of summoning help, more forms of social surveillance, and engrossing activities that undermine forms of alienation that lead to crime. Another possible candidate is psychiatric medication, which has promoted an increased access to mental health services, particularly among males and less educated segments of the population including youth who were reluctant to engage in counseling therapy. These medications may have eased some of the forms of depression, anxiety and hyperactivity that fueled bullying, crime and other deviance.

One implication concerns how bullying and peer victimization are discussed in both the media and the public. Given that surveys continue to show high rates of peer victimization and bullying, and that youth are the most criminally victimized segment of the population, strong concern about this exposure is clearly warranted. But these concerns should not be framed as a recent increase in the problem. Moreover, reporting about the high rates should be tempered with information about the declines.

What should media and researchers say about the size of the decline? Though the various studies point to declines, the magnitudes do vary among the studies. For example, the NCVS showed drops of over 50% in school-related violence since the 1990s, but other studies like the YRBS have declines more like 25%. The NCVS is clearly the oldest and most methodologically rigorous study, but it is not conducted in schools, and its definitions of violence are narrow. If room is not available to cite specific studies, we suggest a formulation such as the following:

> "Studies tracking school violence and bullying since the early 1990s through 2010 show declines of between 25% and 75% for problems such as violent peer victimization, fighting in school, bullying, and school theft."

Another implication concerns how to look at prevention efforts. The trends suggest that something has been helping to reduce the toll of violence and bullying in schools. While we cannot conclude that everything that schools have been doing is contributing positively to this decline, the improvement at least counsels caution about abandoning programs and approaches that have been utilized in the recent past.

The decline also has implications for research and evaluation. In doing program evaluation, it is not sufficient simply to track bullying rates before and after the implementation of a program. If bullying is declining in most places because of some larger social factors, the decline showing up in the evaluation may be due to those factors, not the program being implemented. The proper design is to make sure that the evaluation tracks bullying in some comparison group that is not receiving the program, so the effects for the program group can be distinguished from general overall trends.

Bullying and peer victimization appear to be declining since the 1990s. This is good news. But it should not be interpreted as the problem having been solved. First, the rates are still incredibly high. For example, more than one in 10 high school students said they were in a physical fight on school property in the last year. We would not tolerate a level of workplace danger that was so high, nor should we. Second, there is no reason to assume that the trend will continue downward. It may decline further as we continue to promote violence prevention. But it may also be that the early declines were the easiest, preventing the most readily preventable cases. New strategies and more intensive work may be needed to prevent the parts of the problem that remain.

But advocates and young people should feel inspired. Change can happen, and it can get better.

"Labeled abnormal because it's unfashionable, homeschooling is actually the historical norm, which always involved educating and socializing children at home."

Government Plan to Stop School Shootings: Monitor Homeschoolers

Selwyn Duke

Selwyn Duke is a writer and public speaker. In the following viewpoint, Duke reports that the advisory committee formed following the school shooting at Sandy Hook Elementary School in 2012 recommended more monitoring of homeschool students to prevent further violence. Duke argues that this ruling makes little sense, since most school shootings are not committed by homeschoolers. He also says that homeschoolers are generally more mature and more advanced than public school students. He concludes that public schools encourage dangerous gang-like behavior, in comparison to the healthy, traditional values of homeschooling.

As you read, consider the following questions:

1. Why does Duke believe that the government has a vested interest in eliminating homeschooling?

2. What evidence does Duke provide that homeschoolers are better adjusted and higher achieving than public school students?

3. On what grounds does Duke criticize the public school focus on self-esteem?

A government advisory commission assembled in the wake of the tragic Sandy Hook shooting has issued a proposal for preventing similar events that is raising eyebrows: Monitor certain homeschoolers.

The Sandy Hook Advisory Commission (SHAC), consisting of 16 educators, local and state officials, and "behavioral experts," was created 18 months ago by Governor Dannel Malloy after 20-year-old Adam Lanza committed the Connecticut mass shooting that transfixed the nation in December 2012. Lanza, "described as being 'dark and disturbed' before his death . . . coldly murdered his own mother in their expensive home near Newtown, Connecticut. Then he took her legally registered guns to the nearby Sandy Hook Elementary School and shot and killed 20 children and six adults. Then he took a handgun and shot himself," writes WND.com, describing the chain of events. The commission is targeting homeschooling apparently because Lanza's mother removed him from the government school system in 10th grade and taught him at home for one and a half years.

The SHAC's "chief recommendation"—which is for "tighter scrutiny of homeschoolers"—would only apply to home-educated students labeled with "emotional, social, or behavioral problems." But observers worry this will be used as a pretext for gratuitous state intrusion into homeschooling families, as those with "problem" children "would have to file progress reports prepared by [government] special education program teams," reports CTPost.com. Of special concern is the matter of who will determine what constitutes "emotional, social, or behavioral problems."

This is especially relevant since anti-homeschooling forces have spread the notion that the practice stunts emotional, social, and behavioral development. For example, as Michael F. Haverluck reported at CBN News in 2007, "92 percent of [school] superintendents believe that home learners are emotionally unstable, deprived of proper social development and too judgmental of the world around them, according to a California study by researcher Dr. Brian Ray."

The above statistic relates to another reason many are concerned about the proposal: Government educators have a vested interest in eliminating homeschooling. Every child taught at home means one less student who can be indoctrinated by schools—and means less funding for them.

Observers also point out that not only is placing an onus on homeschoolers based on one anecdote unfair, but Lanza attended government school for the first 10 years of his life; moreover, there are more anecdotes indicating that SHAC's proposed cure is worse than (or may actually be) the disease. As Kyle Olson writes at Education Action Group News:

> [I]f the act of homeschooling and the perceived lack of governmental oversight is to blame, how does Sandy Hook advisory panel explain away these public school students:
>
> • On March 21, 2005, Red Lake Senior High School student Jeffrey Weise killed five students, one teacher, one security guard, and then committed suicide.
>
> • On April 20, 1999, Columbine High School students Eric Harris and Dylan Klebold killed 12 students and one teacher, and wounded 21 others before committing suicide.

- On March 5, 2001, student Charles Andrew Williams killed two students and wounded 13 others at Santana High School in California.

- On February 27, 2012, TJ Lane walked into the Chardon High School cafeteria and fired into a group of students sitting at a lunch table. Three students died in the attack. His "emotional disability" was such that he wore a t-shirt with "Killer" scrawled on it to his sentencing. The examples go on and they all point back to a failed government bureaucracy that apparently didn't adequately address the "behavioral and emotional disabilities" of the students in its care.

More significantly, studies and statistics tell the same tale. As CBN's Haverluck also reported:

Dr. Thomas Smedley ... conducted a study in which he administered the Vineland Adaptive Behavior Scales test to identify mature and well-adapted behaviors in children. Home learners ranked in the 84th percentile, compared to publicly schooled students, who were drastically lower in the 23rd.

... Research presented at the National Christian Home Educators Leadership Conference divulged that homeschool graduates far exceeded their public and private school counterparts in college by ranking the highest in 42 of 63 indicators of collegiate success. They were also ranked as being superior in four out of five achievement categories, including socialization, as they were assessed as being the most charismatic and influential.

... When the Direct Observation Form of the Child Behavior Checklist was administered by education researcher Dr. Larry Shyers to identify 97 problematic behaviors in two groups of children, traditionally schooled students exuded eight times as many antisocial traits than [sic] their homeschooled counterparts.

Homeschooling Socialization

So why the big fuss over socialization? Rather than being related to any real problem homeschooled children have meeting and mingling with fellow humans, it seems to be a problem with the thinking of some adults. These folks think it's "weird" that families would have the audacity to decide for themselves with whom, where, when, and how much or how little "socialization" occurs. The converse of this, of course, is that someone outside the family decides these things for our children. Thus, in recent history, it has been decided that children's socialization occurs in the institution of school, away from the rest of the world, much as the prison institution keeps inmates away from the rest of the world. And the constancy and intensity with which this decision is defended, mostly by those with a vested interest (read paycheck!) in making sure the institution stays full, is cause for pause. This focus on school as children's socialization device is an even more recent invention than public school itself.

What can we learn from this? That (a) the educational decision makers believe the public school system's job extends beyond teaching academics; (b) these same decision makers need a strong criticism of a growing educational alternative that bypasses their control; or (c) both of the above.

Linda Dobson,
The Homeschooling Book of Answers:
The 101 Most Important Questions Answered
by Homeschooling's Most Respected Voice.
New York: Three Rivers Press, 2002.

This will come as no surprise to homeschooling families, whose children figure prominently in national spelling and geography bees and other academic competitions. Labeled abnormal because it's unfashionable, homeschooling is actually the historical norm, which always involved educating and socializing children at home and provides the balance of intense exposure to not just peers (siblings), but also adults such as parents, grandparents, and perhaps extended family. This provides more, and more frequent, modeling of mature adult behavior, and virtues are caught more than they're taught. What is in reality abnormal is the government-school environment, in which children spend much of the day, five days a week, around 30 immature age-mates. In such a setting, a gang-culture-like milieu generally develops, with students influenced more by bad-apple bad boys than the boy wonders; just consider how the pursuit of academic excellence in the black community can be stigmatized as "acting white" or how, anywhere, a well-behaved, diligent student may be mocked as a "goody-goody."

And the proof is in the pudding, say critics. As Haverluck wrote, "The mass socialization conducted within schools has brought about a proliferation of delinquent behavior within this nation's youth, reports education researcher Dr. Michael Slavinski. He notes that student bodies are increasingly riddled with violence, drugs, promiscuity, emotional disorders, crime, contempt for authority, desperate behavior, illiteracy and peer dependency—just to name a few."

Given the clash of the homeschooling and government-schooling worldviews, each of which considers the other abnormal, there's good reason to fear that homeschooler status alone may often be enough to get one labeled "disordered." After all, the two views disagree profoundly on what constitutes proper "socialization." While homeschoolers are often believing Christians who seek to instill godly virtues in their children, "Education researcher Dr. Michael Mitchell found that being popular, aggressively competitive, materialistically driven and self-confident are traits promoted in conventional schools," wrote Haverluck.

In particular, while "[h]ome educators examined by Mitch-ell strive to dismantle any selfish ambitions and self-aggrandizement seen in their children, as opposed to cultivat-ing them," government schools stress "self-esteem." As to this, the self-esteem movement began decades ago with the notion that girls were faltering in school (not true at the time, actually) and that this was due to their having lower self-esteem than boys do. Overlooked, however, was that the high-est scores on self-esteem tests and the lowest academic scores were both registered by the same group: black males. Explana-tion?

"Self-esteem" has simply become a euphemism for pride.

This is why a government-school student may be told he's "the most important person in the world" or be instructed to expound upon his own greatness. But, critics might say, aca-demia today is producing anything but greatness—except in ego. And if "pride goeth before a fall," is it any surprise Ameri-can schooling is falling fast?

Periodical and Internet Sources Bibliography

The following articles have been selected to supplement the diverse views presented in this chapter.

Emma Brown	"U.S. Public Schools Report Fewer Violent Incidents," *Washington Post*, May 21, 2015.
Maureen Downey	"Teens on Violence, Bullying: Half of High School Boys Admit to Hitting Out of Anger," *Atlanta Journal-Constitution* (Georgia), November 4, 2013.
Andrew Dunn	"Are Charter Schools Safer?," *Charlotte Observer* (North Carolina), April 3, 2014.
Kerry Fehr-Snyder	"Charter-School Safety a Concern," *Arizona Republic*, January 29, 2013.
Michelle Goldberg	"The Sinister Side of Homeschooling," Daily Beast, September 20, 2013.
Josh Israel	"'Anonymous Tip': Homeschooling's Obsession with 'False' Reports of Child Abuse," *ThinkProgress*, September 10, 2014.
Stacy Teicher Khadaroo	"Bullying Declines in US Schools as More Students Embrace Diversity, Tolerance," *Christian Science Monitor*, May 15, 2015.
Andrew Adam Newman	"The Fight Against Bullying in Schools Expands to Store Shelves," *New York Times*, September 30, 2013.
Peter K. Smith and Fran Thompson	"The Best Way to Stop Bullying: Get the Cool Kids to Stick Up for the Victims," *Washington Post*, August 8, 2014.
Greg Toppo	"Schools Safe as Ever Despite Spate of Shootings, Scares," *USA Today*, November 13, 2013.

OPPOSING
VIEWPOINTS®
SERIES

CHAPTER 2

Can Better Gun Policy Make Schools Safer?

Chapter Preface

Gun control activists have long argued that the best way to reduce gun violence is to reduce access to guns. Gun rights advocates, though, often believe that gun violence could be reduced, not by outlawing guns, but by improving knowledge of gun safety. This has resulted in the controversial idea that gun safety should be taught in schools.

South Carolina Republican lawmaker Alan Clemmons, for example, proposed a measure in the South Carolina state legislature in January 2015 that would establish gun classes in South Carolina schools. The class would be a three-week course designed by the National Rifle Association of America (NRA). "One result of hostility toward the Second Amendment has been an absolute intolerance for any discussion of guns or depiction of guns in writing or in assignments in public schools, which is an affront to First Amendment rights and harshly inhibits creative expression and academic freedom," Clemmons said, according to a January 2015 article at MSNBC.com.

Opinions are mixed on whether gun classes would actually reduce gun violence. Maine Republican state legislator Paul Davis wanted high school students to learn about guns to ensure they can handle firearms correctly. "I'm not asking you to have teachers armed, and I'm not asking that signs saying gun-free zones be removed. I'm not asking for any of that," Davis said in an article at TakePart. "I only want the children and the students to have a chance to learn about guns and how they work as well as how to be safe with them."

Others are skeptical that gun safety programs would be effective. Two 2004 studies found that gun safety programs for children do little good and can even increase the likelihood the children will handle guns unsafely. Steve Albrecht, a gun safety expert, argues that gun safety classes do not reduce violence, but that schools can contribute to gun safety by reaching out to parents and making sure they understand the importance of keeping guns out of the reach of children. "Part of the issue has to be educating the parents to keep the guns secure first. Because it doesn't matter if the kids have been to a gun safety program or not," he said in an article for CNN.

The viewpoints in the following chapter examine other issues surrounding gun policy and schools, including whether gun control can increase school safety and the possibility of passing gun control legislation.

> *"Beyond the headlines there is a steady
> daily tally of violence that is mainly ig-
> nored in the press."*

Gun Control Can Prevent School Shootings

Matt Bennett

*Matt Bennett is cofounder and senior vice president for public
affairs of Third Way; he served as an adviser on gun policy to
Sandy Hook Promise, an organization that advocates mental
health and wellness as it relates to gun safety. In the following
viewpoint, Bennett discusses his work with the families of the
children killed in the 2012 Sandy Hook Elementary School shooting. The families are lobbying for gun control legislation to re-
strict firearm sales and to close loopholes that allow people to obtain guns at gun shows or online without having background
checks. Bennett says that the legislative process is very difficult
because of strong opposition from the gun lobby. However, he believes that the Sandy Hook families can help make legislation
possible and that better gun control laws can reduce gun violence.*

As you read, consider the following questions:

1. What are some possible sources of the American passion for guns, according to Bennett?

2. According to the viewpoint, who is Wayne LaPierre, and what is his importance in the gun control debate?

3. Why is Bennett hopeful, even though the Sandy Hook families failed to get legislation passed?

It was the saddest roll call I've ever heard. "I'm Nelba; my daughter's name is Ana; she was six." "I'm Mark; my son's name was Daniel; he was seven." "I'm Nicole; my son's name is Dylan; he's six."

Sandy Hook Families for Gun Control

And on it went, as we sat around the table of a sterile conference room at a DC law firm, the confused and confusing mix of tenses signaling the freshness of loss, the impossibility of comprehending it yet. It was late January 2013, barely a month after the mass shooting at Sandy Hook Elementary School, and these were the families of some of the victims. Eleven of them had somehow summoned the strength to come to Washington to meet privately with Vice President [Joe] Biden, members of Congress and cabinet members. But they weren't here simply to accept high-level condolences. They had come to listen and to learn about mental health and school safety policy. And they were preparing to wade into some of the roughest waters in American politics: the gun debate.

I was there to help them navigate those waters. The families' DC-based advisor had invited my organization, Third Way—a group deeply involved with efforts to change the gun laws—to give them a sense of what they were in for.

At that moment, with teddy bears still adorning makeshift shrines all over Newtown, [Connecticut,] it seemed that progress on gun safety would be inevitable. President [Barack]

Obama had given a resolute speech in Connecticut vowing to fight for change, and members of Congress seemed to be reacting more like parents than politicians. Senator Joe Manchin, a gun-owning Democrat from West Virginia, said on television what many Americans were saying at their kitchen tables: "They are killing our babies; this has got to stop."

As Joe Manchin knew, however, it was never going to be that simple. Time and again, high-profile gun crimes—from assassinations to mass shootings—had seemed to galvanize public opinion. Yet time and again, this sense of urgency had faded, as the gun lobby slowed momentum in Congress to a crawl and then, often, to a halt.

I stood before the Sandy Hook families on that day in January to brief them on the basics of gun policy and politics. These are smart, educated people. They assumed that, in the wake of this horror, Congress would pass some long-overdue gun safety measures. By then, however, this much was already clear to the political classes: There wasn't going to be a renewed ban on assault weapons or high-capacity ammunition magazines, no matter how wrenching the scene in Newtown. Congress just didn't have the courage to take such a step. The Senate wouldn't pass it, and the House wouldn't even consider it.

When I broke this news to the families, one of the mothers let me know, gently but firmly, that I had screwed up. "Don't tell us what can't be done, because we just aren't prepared to hear that," she said. "Tell us that it could take time, which we can accept, because we're in this for the long haul. And tell us what we *can* do *now* to honor the memory of our children."

The Sandy Hook Promise

Never before had the families of the victims of a gun massacre come together with such a focused commitment to bring about legislative and social change to Washington. The group

I was meeting with, Sandy Hook Promise (SHP), had gotten its start in Newtown in the days after the murders. It began as a gathering in one family's kitchen, with grief-stricken friends and neighbors of the victims vowing to support their community and to do something good for the country in the wake of such an overwhelming tragedy. Their "promise" was to listen and to learn, to promote dialogue, and to pursue "common sense solutions" in the areas of mental health, school safety and gun responsibility.

Staffed by a sea of volunteers from Newtown and led by a few business professionals who took leave from their jobs to run it, SHP grew with astonishing speed into a sophisticated, effective organization. They enlisted a highly respected Washington consultant, Ricki Seidman, to guide them, and she quickly assembled a team of advisors. Within weeks of the funerals, the staff and volunteers from the community, along with many of the victims' families themselves, were already working the corridors of power in Hartford. Eventually, they partnered with Governor Dannel Malloy on a strong new gun safety bill for Connecticut that flew through the legislature and was signed into law less than three months after the murders. At the same time, they began coming to Washington, where they were hoping to achieve a similar result in Congress.

Tim Makris, the father of a Sandy Hook Elementary fourth grader who was not hurt in the shootings, is a cofounder of SHP and runs it day to day. He and the other leaders of SHP were building the ship as it sailed, putting together an office, staffing it with volunteers, raising money, hiring consultants, tending to the many needs of the Sandy Hook community, and providing a support group for families of the victims as well as for those they call the "survivors"—the 12 kids who made it out alive from the two classrooms that were under attack.

At the same time, Makris and the others, including some of the victims' families themselves, were getting a crash course on Senate procedure, gun policy and, most of all, gun politics. They were beginning to appreciate the degree of moral authority they would wield in this debate—and also the severe limits on this unwanted new power. . . .

So Many Guns in America, So Many Ways to Get Them

The question of how to make the country safer from the carnage of gun violence is vital, because the assassinations and mass murders that galvanize our attention every so often actually account for only a small percentage of gun-related deaths. Beyond the headlines there is a steady daily tally of violence that is mainly ignored in the press. The total number of gun deaths per year is about 31,000. This includes roughly 11,400 murders, 19,000 suicides and 600 accidental shootings—more than 10 firearms deaths per 100,000 people every year. By contrast, Japan, which has strict gun control laws, has 0.07 per 100,000, and Switzerland, where most citizens have guns in the home, has 3.84. In addition to deaths, the U.S. has about 80,000 firearms-related injuries annually and 500,000 crimes involving a firearm every year—about one per minute.

Because there is no national database of guns or gun owners, no one knows how many guns are in private hands in the U.S. According to polling, the rate of gun ownership (the percentage of households containing one or more firearms) has actually been falling over the last two decades, but the total number of guns in private possession has gone up sharply, from 200 million in 1994 to somewhere between 270 and 300 million today.

When we compare ourselves to other countries (using the latest data, from the 2007 Small Arms Survey), we find that the U.S. has by far the highest rate of private gun ownership in the world: 88 guns per 100 people. (Next on the list is Yemen, at 55 guns per 100.) At the conservative estimate of 270 million guns, Americans have stockpiled almost half of the privately owned firearms in the world.

The overwhelming majority of those guns are in the possession of responsible, law-abiding adults. But that leaves plenty that are not. The question confronting lawmakers is how to stop a legal product from getting into the hands of those who would use it for illegal purposes.

The answer begins with understanding where criminals get their guns, and we actually know a lot about that. First, in 90 percent of gun crimes, the firearm has changed hands at least once since the original sale, meaning that someone other than the first dealer provided the gun to the criminal. Second, about one-third of the guns involved in crime have crossed state lines, despite the federal prohibition against moving guns interstate. Third, the most common age of those who commit crimes with guns is 19, followed by 20, followed by 18, despite the fact that licensed dealers are not permitted to sell handguns to anyone under 21 (and virtually all gun crimes are committed with handguns). Taken together, these data suggest that crime guns tend to come from an interstate network of gun traffickers that moves guns out of the legal market and into the hands of criminals and minors. The traffickers who provide these crime guns get them from dealers (often through the use of "straw" purchasers who go through the background check for others), from theft, or from unregulated "private sales" at gun shows or through the Internet.

The patterns and sources of crime gun trafficking have been well known for a long time. Then representative [Chuck] Schumer was issuing reports about the so-called "iron highway" of black-market firearms as far back as 1996. But his was a lonely voice, and few put any effort into erecting roadblocks to stem the flow of this traffic.

The massacre at Columbine High School in 1999 changed that by spotlighting a main on-ramp to this highway: gun shows. One of the guns used by those underage killers was obtained for them by a girlfriend who was unaware of their plan. She bought it from an unlicensed seller at a gun show, and after the attack she testified that she would not have gone through with the transaction had she been asked to submit to a background check. . . .

A Burning Passion for Guns

Because of what they have gone through, you would assume that the Sandy Hook families would be greeted with universal demonstrations of respect, kindness and sympathy, even by those who disagree with the legislative goals they are pursuing. But you would be wrong. When two of the families went to Hartford for a state legislative hearing in late January, some gun rights proponents made national news by heckling Neil Heslin, whose son Jesse was killed in the massacre. Dozens of activists in the crowd shouted "Second Amendment!" as Heslin testified.

The outbursts in the Connecticut capitol drew widespread opprobrium. Yet this was hardly the worst of what the families have suffered at the hands of some gun rights supporters. Indeed, a full-fledged conspiracy theory was hatched in the fevered fantasies of some Second Amendment absolutists. They accused the families of creating a "hoax," of faking the deaths of their children and adult loved ones. Facebook pages and YouTube channels were launched to "prove" this proposition. And some of the families received calls, e-mails and letters insisting that they were actors and liars, playing their part in an Obama-led scheme to abrogate gun rights.

This harassment of families in the midst of their deepest grief added a new level of barbarity to the debate over guns in America. And it made clear that for some, guns are a flashpoint in our politics that burns as hot as anything we have seen since the civil rights movement.

It is not clear where all of this passion comes from, because the headwaters of the American gun culture have never been discovered. It could be our frontier spirit; it could be our libertarian ethos; it could be the Second Amendment itself. Whatever the source, Americans in much of the country have developed the belief that gun ownership is somewhere on the continuum between being a legal privilege and a nearly sacred right.

Approximately 100 million adults live in a home with a gun. (The term "gun owner" can be slippery when it comes to family-owned firearms.) They break down roughly into three groups: those who own guns mainly for sport, those who own guns for protection, and those who own guns as a bulwark against government tyranny.

Numerous polls show that the overwhelming majority of people in the first two groups (sport shooters and home protectors) are comfortable with the kinds of commonsense restrictions on gun ownership advocated by the Sandy Hook parents. The third group, however, is made up of what we could call the "constitutionalists." Though a distinct minority, this group has come to control the terms of the gun debate, exercising a power that vastly exceeds their numbers. Their principal mechanism for wielding this power is, of course, the NRA [National Rifle Association of America].

The NRA

The National Rifle Association is nearly 150 years old and claims a membership of 4.5 million. For most of its history, the NRA was a stolid, safety-oriented group. . . . They handed out safe shooter patches to summer campers and worked on land conservation. At the annual NRA convention in 1977, however, the "Cincinnati Revolution" upended those traditions. Constitutionalists ousted the old leadership and installed a new, hard-line regime focused on the absolute protection of gun rights and broader conservative political activism.

Who these constitutionalists are and how many they number we don't know with any certainty. Some are anti-government conspiracy theorists who believe that the "black helicopters" are coming to take their guns. In the 1990s, the most radical of these formed so-called "militias" that refused to pay taxes or honor gun laws. They were the catalyst for the sieges and shootings at Ruby Ridge [site of a deadly confrontation and siege in northern Idaho in 1992 between a white separatist and federal marshals that resulted in three deaths] and Waco [referring to the siege of a Waco, Texas, compound belonging to a religious group known as the Branch Davidians by federal and state law enforcement and U.S. military in 1993], and they spawned Timothy McVeigh, the main bomber of the Oklahoma City Federal Building in 1995.

While most constitutionalists do not advocate violence, they are resolute about gun rights and gun ownership. They believe that gun laws actually make communities less safe by disarming the good guys. Post-Newtown, this was reflected in the NRA's central proposal, which was to put armed guards in schools and to give teachers gun training. And they reject any gun safety measure, no matter how small, as a Second Amendment violation. When they join the NRA, the constitutionalists subscribe not to *American Rifleman*, the NRA's magazine for mainstream sport shooters; they get *America's 1st Freedom*, the NRA's hard-line journal for its most committed core.

By 1991, when staff lobbyist Wayne LaPierre ascended to the post of executive vice president, the NRA had become the uncompromising political behemoth we know today. LaPierre has remained in power ever since, while the more ceremonial post of NRA president has rotated. Sometimes they have camera-ready presidents like Charlton Heston; at the moment they have James Porter, an ultraconservative Alabama lawyer who calls the Civil War "the War of Northern Aggression."

The NRA under LaPierre has never deviated from its goals, never softened its tone, no matter what the context. Only seven months after 9/11 [referring to the September 11, 2001, terrorist attacks on the United States], LaPierre gave a speech at the NRA convention where he attacked Americans for Gun Safety [AGS] for trying to "hijack your freedom and take a box-cutter to the Constitution." "That's political terrorism," he thundered, "and it's a far greater threat to your freedom than any foreign force."

The NRA's political bullying extends beyond its rhetoric. When AGS recruited [U.S. senator] John McCain to work with us on the gun show loophole legislation, the NRA turned on him. Despite his previous A-rating, the NRA attacked him publicly and threatened him with political war in private. They've done the same with countless other lawmakers, and they have made enemies; former president George H.W. Bush quit the group in disgust in 1995 when LaPierre called federal agents "jack-booted thugs . . . wearing Nazi helmets and black storm trooper uniforms."

Similar bullying—of friends who don't toe the line—occurs even within the gun industry. When the iconic firearms manufacturer Smith & Wesson agreed to a deal with the [Bill] Clinton administration on the issue of trigger locks, the NRA called for a boycott. Smith & Wesson sales dropped 40 percent, after which the company went private, fired its management and abrogated its agreement with the White House.

The gun industry's trade association, the National Shooting Sports Foundation [NSSF], has followed the NRA's lead on all things political. As a result, the NSSF has refused to endorse the Senate gun safety bill. That might not be surprising if it weren't for one fact: the NSSF headquarters is in Newtown, Connecticut—less than three miles from Sandy Hook Elementary School.

Sandy Hook Families: Still in the Arena

In the months between the Sandy Hook shootings and the April gun bill debate in the Senate, Joe Biden and Chuck Schumer were back in the saddle again, working to cut a deal

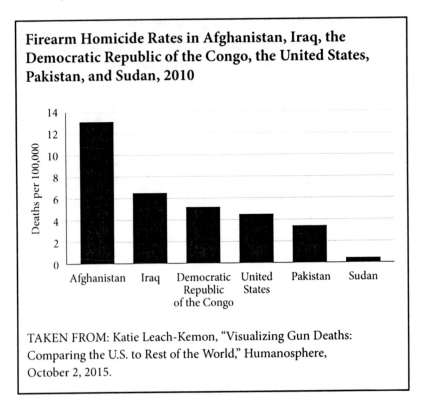

Firearm Homicide Rates in Afghanistan, Iraq, the Democratic Republic of the Congo, the United States, Pakistan, and Sudan, 2010

TAKEN FROM: Katie Leach-Kemon, "Visualizing Gun Deaths: Comparing the U.S. to Rest of the World," *Humanosphere*, October 2, 2015.

that could survive an NRA onslaught. From the White House, the vice president was corralling the gun safety groups, coaxing the lawmakers and cajoling the public. In the Senate, Schumer was running the inside game, trying to find an NRA-approved Republican to make a match with his NRA-friendly Democrat, Joe Manchin.

On the eve of the Senate debate, they succeeded. Pat Toomey, a conservative Pennsylvania Republican, agreed to cosponsor legislation with Manchin that would close the gun show and Internet loopholes. The announcement of the Manchin-Toomey amendment helped overcome a filibuster, with 16 Republicans joining most Democrats in voting to proceed to the debate.

That week, Tim Makris and a sizable group of SHP families were in town to lobby. The level of their newfound sophistication about Washington and gun policy was impressive. After they were briefed on the contents of Manchin-Toomey, they immediately began pressing target senators to support the bill. They were told time and again that the bill would never have progressed this far without them and that they had much to be proud of.

It's often the case that some of the most effective advocates in American politics are people who have a personal stake in an issue. Those seeking funding for serious diseases, including nearly every variety of cancer, have perfected the art of cause-based lobbying. They bring people who are suffering from the illness, photos of family members lost to it, testimonials to the pain and misery endured by their loved ones, and PowerPoints replete with statistics and data. They are routinely granted audiences with congressional staff members to make their case.

But it is a rare thing for such advocates to be granted time with almost any senator they ask to meet—rarer still for them to be able to move even the most jaded of these lawmakers to tears by bringing out a photo of a smiling six-year-old child. Yet that keeps happening with the Sandy Hook families. Vice President Biden has remarked that it is impossible to meet with these families and not become emotional "unless you're made of stone." Indeed, almost every meeting they do results in senators and members of Congress weeping as they hear the stories of Newtown.

But these families don't want sympathy. They want a bill signed into law, and that was not to be—at least not yet. Mounting a furious lobbying campaign, the NRA held onto all but four Republicans and enough wayward Democrats (four) that the final 54–46 tally on April 17 fell six votes short of the threshold necessary to send the amendment on for a majority-rules, up-or-down vote.

Public reaction has been swift and surprising. For the first time in the modern history of the debate, a gun safety vote has had a negative impact on the approval rating of senators voting "no" (even in red and purple states like Alaska, Arizona and New Hampshire) and a positive impact on red-state senators voting "yes" (Louisiana and North Carolina).

In that political shift, there is hope. Most of those who voted "no" surely know that they did the wrong thing by opposing the expansion of background checks in commercial settings. If they believe they erred not just morally and substantively but politically, they will change. Many are pushing them to do so, including New York mayor Michael Bloomberg and his group Mayors Against Illegal Guns, which brings deep policy expertise and massive financial resources to the fight. Others, including Vice President Biden, Senators Manchin and Schumer, former representative Gabby Giffords [who was shot in the head from near point-blank range at an event in Tucson, AZ] and her group Americans for Responsible Solutions, Third Way, the Center for American Progress, and the Brady Campaign [to Prevent Gun Violence], are also pressing the case.

Still in the arena as well are the families of Sandy Hook. Despite the glare of a spotlight that has forced them to repeatedly relive their darkest hour and subjected them to a stunning level of personal vitriol, they continue to come to Washington, meet with senators and talk to the press. They accepted early on that this was a long road—that a 20-year gridlock on gun policy was not likely to change in an instant.

The motto of Sandy Hook Promise is "Our hearts are broken; Our spirit is not." And the extraordinary generosity of spirit that these brave people bring to this nasty, brutish political debate could, in the end, make all the difference.

"Gun control laws do not correlate with less violence."

Gun Control Won't Prevent School Shootings

John G. Malcolm and Jennifer A. Marshall

John G. Malcolm is a senior legal fellow and Jennifer A. Marshall is director of domestic policy studies, both at the Heritage Foundation. In the following viewpoint, they argue that gun control decisions need to be made carefully and must be in accordance with Second Amendment constitutional rights to bear arms. They say that the Supreme Court has determined that many gun control laws are unconstitutional. They also argue that research has not linked more gun control with less violence. They suggest that reducing mass shootings requires local and cultural solutions, not national gun control.

As you read, consider the following questions:

1. What recommendations do the authors make about addressing cultural issues to reduce gun violence?

2. What did the Supreme Court say to the notion that the Second Amendment is outmoded?

3. Who was Gary Kleck, and how does his story point to the danger of too strict gun control laws, in the view of the authors?

In responding to horrific crimes such as the massacre in Newtown, Connecticut [referring to the Sandy Hook Elementary School shooting], individuals, families, civil society, and possibly government must channel their concerns into effective measures that are consistent with the Constitution. As we try to make society safer and stronger, constitutional and complex cultural factors must be taken into consideration, and sound policy must be based on a serious study of the data and other evidence. Policy makers should avoid a rush to judgment on prescriptions that violate first principles, ignore the real root of these complex problems, or disregard careful social science research. Any federal government role must be limited and constrained by constitutional principles. The most important solutions lie at the state and local levels, in the community and within the family.

Careful Policy

All Americans, from whatever walks of life and of whatever political or philosophical convictions, abhor the death of innocent human beings and had a visceral reaction of shock and pain to the killing of 20 schoolchildren and six staff members in Newtown, Connecticut, in December 2012. In responding to this attack, Americans must consider with great reflection and care how best to proceed, in a manner consistent with our laws and our traditions, to protect innocent lives.

First, we must identify the specific problems to be addressed involving school safety, mental illness, the cultural climate, and the misuse of firearms.

Second, we must analyze potential solutions to the specific problems identified, examining the facts and taking into account the costs and benefits of the potential solutions to ensure that sound judgment governs the emotions inescapably attached to the subject.

Finally, Americans must implement appropriate solutions in a manner that is consistent with the Constitution, including the Second Amendment guarantee of the right to keep and bear arms, the traditional role of the states in our federal system, and the central significance of family.

Making public policy is especially challenging in these circumstances. In responding to tragedies such as Newtown, concern must be channeled by individuals, families, civil society, and possibly government into effective measures that are consistent with the Constitution. Policy makers should not just do *something* to alleviate our sense of urgent responsibility without due consideration of its effects. Careful diagnosis of the full scope of the problem is essential. Complex cultural factors must be taken into consideration, and sober judgment about human nature is required. Constitutional principles and constraints, which are so vital to preserving our cherished liberties, must be observed. Not all problems can be solved with government action, and if government action is required, any federal action, including executive orders, should be consistent with our federal system of government, respect for state sovereignty, and the separation of powers.

Our Constitution was framed for a self-governing people, and effective constitutional responses will therefore transcend federal policy mechanisms. Policy makers should avoid rushing to judgment on prescriptions that fail to respect constitutional principle or to locate the root of the problems, some of which lie in complex cultural issues that are best addressed at the state and local levels or that lie beyond the reach of policy altogether—best addressed by families, religious congregations, and other institutions of civil society.

Principles to Follow

In addressing the topics of gun laws, school safety, mental health, and cultural issues, Americans should focus on the following principles:

Respecting the Right to Keep and Bear Arms: The constitutional right to keep and bear arms is an individual right that is fundamental to a free society, which depends, ultimately, on personal responsibility.

- The Second Amendment continues to be an important safeguard of Americans' security.

- Gun control laws do not correlate with decreased violence.

Preserving School Safety: Since a number of shootings have occurred on public school grounds in recent years, the safety of students on campus is a priority concern.

- Decisions about school security are quintessentially matters that are the responsibility of state and local governments.

- Community-level identification of and response to risks is essential.

Addressing Mental Illness: While there is no clear evidence that people with severe mental illnesses who are being treated are more dangerous than the general population, it is clear that some with severe illnesses who are not being treated are more dangerous.

- Decisions about addressing the risks of school violence arising from mental illness are state and local responsibilities.

- States can both reduce the risk of school violence and address mental illness humanely.

Addressing Cultural Issues: Citizens, parents, and cultural norms may be more important than anything else in working to prevent the recurrence of tragedies such as Newtown.

- Family plays an essential role in developing thriving children and adolescents, and its role must be respected in policy and supported in communities.

- Civil society institutions offer a first line of defense in building and maintaining safe and thriving communities.

- The First Amendment's protection of freedom of speech means that it is up to individuals, families, communities, and corporations to make responsible choices regarding media production and consumption.

Violent episodes like that in Newtown shatter the well-being of a community and unsettle the peace of mind that Americans typically enjoy. Responses must seek to restore the protection afforded by the rule of law and a thriving civil society of individuals exercising their responsibilities as citizens and community members.

The Right to Keep and Bear Arms

The Second Amendment continues to be an important safeguard of Americans' security. The Constitution's Second Amendment provides that, "A well regulated Militia, being necessary to the security of a free State, the right of the people to keep and bear Arms, shall not be infringed." In 2008, in *[District of Columbia] v. Heller*, the Supreme Court of the United States held that the Second Amendment protects a right of individuals to keep and bear arms, not just a right to arms only in service of a government-organized militia such as the National Guard. In 2010, in *McDonald v. Chicago*, the court held that this is a fundamental right that also applies against state and local governments.

The founding generation did not trust standing armies. As Justice Antonin Scalia noted in his majority opinion in *Heller*, English history is replete with instances in which monarchs "succeeded in using select militias loyal to them to suppress political dissidents, in part by disarming their opponents," just as King George III tried to do with the colonists in areas he considered rebellious. This provoked a reaction by the colonists, who invoked their well-established rights as Englishmen to keep their firearms.

The Revolutionary War, however, had made it clear that militia forces alone could not be relied upon to provide an adequate national defense, so the founders decided to give the federal government authority to establish standing armies, including in peacetime. They recognized, though, that this posed a threat to liberty, especially in light of the fact that the proposed Constitution also forbade the states from keeping troops without the consent of Congress. While the federalists and the anti-federalists debated whether federal control of the militia would take away from the states their principal means of defense against federal oppression, both sides assumed that the federal government did not and should not have any authority to disarm the citizenry any more than it should have the power to abridge the freedom of speech or prohibit the free exercise of religion.

Apart from the Second Amendment's role in deterring government oppression, however, the right to keep and bear arms has another purpose that is every bit as important and urgent today as it was at the time the Constitution was ratified: specifically, to enable American citizens to defend themselves against violent criminals. Even a model police force is not everywhere at all times, and response times for many police departments leave citizens vulnerable for long periods. The founders accepted the individual right of self-defense as the natural basis for the right to arms. They were no doubt influenced by natural law theorists such as William Black-

Defensive Guns

While news stories sometimes chronicle the defensive uses of guns, such discussions are rare compared to those depicting violent crime committed with guns. Since in many defensive cases a handgun is simply brandished, and no one is harmed, many defensive uses are never even reported to the police. I believe that this underreporting of defensive gun use is large, and this belief has been confirmed by the many stories I received from people across the country after the publicity broke on my original study. On the roughly one hundred radio talk shows on which I discussed that study, many people called in to say that they believed having a gun to defend themselves with had saved their lives. For instance, on a Philadelphia radio station, a New Jersey woman told how two men simultaneously had tried to open both front doors of the car she was in. When she brandished her gun and yelled, the men backed away and fled. Given the stringent gun control laws in New Jersey, the woman said she never thought seriously of reporting the attempted attack to the police.

John R. Lott Jr., More Guns, Less Crime: Understanding Crime and Gun Control Laws. *3rd ed. Chicago: University of Chicago Press, 2010.*

stone, who said, "Self-defence therefore, as it is justly called the primary law of nature, so it is not, neither can it be in fact, taken away by the law of society." Accordingly, the people who gave us the Second Amendment drew no fundamental distinction between an individual's right to defend himself against a robber and that same individual's right to band together with others in a state-regulated militia.

It is clear that the Second Amendment protects the right of individuals to privately keep and bear their own firearms that are suitable as individual weapons for hunting, sport shooting, self-protection, and other lawful purposes. In *Heller*, the court made clear that while "some think that the Second Amendment is outmoded in a society where our standing army is the pride of our Nation, where well-trained police forces provide personal security, and where gun violence is a serious problem[, . . .] it is not the role of this Court to pronounce the Second Amendment extinct."

What is important to stress as a matter of first principles and now settled constitutional law is (1) that the Second Amendment guarantees fundamental, individual rights of all law-abiding adults and (2) that in seeking to apply the Second Amendment, lawmakers and judges must be faithful to the original public meaning of the Second Amendment as understood at the time of its passage by Congress and ratification by the states, particularly as to the understanding of the natural right of self-defense, rather than some purely pragmatic argument about what legislators and ratifiers would want it to mean today if they were redrafting the Constitution in modern times.

Gun Control Laws Do Not Correlate with Decreased Violence

In addition to the constitutional and philosophical constraints involved in regulating a fundamental right, any laws should be carefully evaluated in light of historical evidence and with a thorough examination of data about their effectiveness.

Concerning the historical evidence on mass killings, Dr. Grant Duwe, a criminologist with the Minnesota Department of Corrections and the author of a book on the history of mass murders in America, states that the rate of mass killings, defined as four or more fatalities in a 24-hour period, peaked (on a per capita basis) in 1929, which was the height of a crime wave and was comprised mainly of familicides [a type of murder in which a spouse and one or more children are killed, followed by suicide of the perpetrator] and felony-related massacres. In terms of mass public shootings unconnected with the commission of another felony, which constitute a little more than 10 percent of all mass murders, the number rose from the 1960s through the 1990s, peaking in 1991 with eight such incidents.

While it is true that the number of victims killed and wounded in mass public shootings was greater in 2012 than in any previous year, there does not appear to be any discernible upward trend in the number of mass shooting incidents. According to Duwe's estimates, 32 mass shootings occurred in the 1980s, 42 in the 1990s, and 26 in the 2000s. Further, while the rate of random mass shootings in the United States has increased over the past 30 years, according to the FBI [Federal Bureau of Investigation], the total U.S. homicide rate has fallen by over half since 1980, and the gun homicide rate has fallen along with it. While gun ownership doubled in the late 20th century, Americans are safer today from "violent crime, including gun homicide, than they have been at any time since the mid-1960s."

Gun ownership does not correlate with increased violence. For example, the rate of gun ownership is higher in rural areas than in urban areas, but the murder rate is higher in urban areas. Similarly, according to one study, blacks are more likely to be victims of violent crimes than whites, but gun ownership among blacks is notably lower than among whites. In localities where right-to-carry laws were enacted, communities saw a decline in murder rates and instances of other violent crimes.

Cross-national and cross-cultural comparisons of gun ownership and violence are notoriously problematic for many reasons, but it is important to note that the correlations do not run in only one direction, as some gun control advocates imply by referencing only a few examples that support their narrative. Gun ownership is roughly three times as high in Switzerland as it is in Germany, yet the Swiss have had lower murder rates. Other countries with high rates of gun ownership and low murder rates include Israel, New Zealand, and Finland.

Between 1940 and the early 1960s, when the use of firearms by dangerous criminals was less prevalent, people could buy guns, ammunition, and dynamite from hardware stores; the Sears Christmas catalog had page upon page of rifles and shotguns that could be ordered through the mail; and some high schools and scout groups had (and in some states still have) shooting teams. Many high school students on those teams kept their rifles in their school lockers. All of this was before the federal Gun Control Act of 1968 was enacted and before background checks and waiting periods were implemented in the 1990s.

No Panacea

Gun control laws do not correlate with decreased violence. If gun control were a panacea, then Washington, D.C., Oakland, and Chicago, which have very strict gun control laws, would be among the safest places to live rather than among the most dangerous. While some countries with strict gun control laws, such as Japan, experience very little violence as a result of criminal use of firearms, other countries, such as Russia, Brazil, and Mexico, have stricter gun control laws but higher per capita rates of violence through the criminal use of guns than the United States does. Joyce Lee Malcolm's work points to the "cautionary tale" of Britain's experience with banning handguns only to see a rise in gun crime.

During the decade that the assault weapons ban was in place, our nation's public schools were subjected to over two dozen incidents of violence through the criminal use of guns—including the Columbine [High School] massacre, in which Eric Harris, 18, and Dylan Klebold, 17, killed 12 students and a teacher before shooting themselves. A study by the University of Pennsylvania, commissioned by the Department of Justice, entitled "An Updated Assessment of the Federal Assault Weapons Ban: Impacts on Gun Markets and Gun Violence, 1994–2003," concluded:

> [W]e cannot clearly credit the ban with any of the nation's recent drop in gun violence. And, indeed, there has been no discernible reduction in the lethality and injuriousness of gun violence, based on indicators like the percentage of gun crimes resulting in death or the share of gunfire incidents resulting in injury. . . .

Moreover, gun bans create vulnerabilities by disarming law-abiding citizens. Professor of criminology Gary Kleck of Florida State University found that the number of defensive gun uses may be as high as 2.1 million to 2.5 million times per year. Additionally, there have been numerous occasions where mass shooters have been stopped before they could continue their mayhem by ordinary citizens with lawfully possessed firearms. Examples include, among others, an assistant principal who stopped Luke Woodham who, after killing his mother at home, killed two students and wounded seven others at a high school in Pearl, Mississippi, in 1997; the dance hall owner who stopped Andrew Wurst after he killed a teacher and wounded three others at an eighth-grade graduation dance in Edinboro, Pennsylvania, in 1998; and, the students who stopped Peter Odighizuwa after he killed a dean, a professor, and a student and wounded three others at Appalachian School of Law in Grundy, Virginia, in 2002.

The Second Amendment's guarantee of the right to keep and bear arms is fundamental to a free society, which depends, ultimately, on personal responsibility. The debate over gun laws must be situated in a larger discussion about the character of our civic order. It should not be used to avoid addressing cultural questions that require much more widespread action on the part of civil society: that is, the personal responsibility of all Americans for their own and their neighbors' good.

> "Advocates needed to send a signal that politicians could vote for gun control without fear of ending their careers. Instead, they sent the opposite message."

Gun Control Legislation Cannot Pass

Molly Ball

Molly Ball is a staff writer for the Atlantic, *covering national politics. In the following viewpoint, Ball reports on recall elections for Colorado state lawmakers who voted for gun control. Gun control supporters were defeated in two instances by vigorous campaigns backed by the National Rifle Association of America. Ball concludes that going forward, politicians will be scared to vote for gun control for fear it will hurt them in elections. Gun control legislation, she says, is therefore impossible to pass.*

As you read, consider the following questions:

1. What arguments do the gun control advocates make that Ball says are true, but which do not matter?

2. What does Ball say that MassEquality did that the gun control lobby has failed to do?

3. According to the viewpoint, what gun control provisions does Matt Bennett argue are still popular in Colorado?

Ever since the Senate voted down gun control legislation in April [2013], some advocates have remained convinced there was still hope. As of Tuesday [in September 2013], that hope is officially dead.

State Senators Recalled

On Tuesday, two Colorado state senators, both Democrats, were recalled by voters for their votes in favor of gun control. Gun rights advocates instigated the recall drives; the National Rifle Association [of America, NRA] spent $360,000, sending mailers and airing television ads calling the lawmakers "too extreme for Colorado." Gun control proponents, buoyed by donations from New York mayor Mike Bloomberg, outspent their opponents five to one. But the NRA turned the money against the lawmakers, painting them as pawns of fancy-pants out-of-state liberal interests. And the NRA won.

Democrats and gun control advocates have come up with a number of rosy rationalizations to minimize the loss. Gun rights campaigners failed to collect enough signatures to initiate two other recalls, they point out, so the victory was really mixed. The gun control laws passed by the Colorado legislature remain in place, and Democrats retain control of both houses. Tuesday's recall was a low-turnout election with procedural irregularities that made it harder for people to vote. Both lawmakers represented tough districts, particularly Senator Angela Giron, whose district was Democratic but culturally conservative; she lost by 12 points, while state senate president John Morse lost by fewer than 400 votes.

All those things are true. And they don't matter.

Here's what matters for the future of gun control: Advocates needed to send a signal that politicians could vote for gun control without fear of ending their careers. Instead, they sent the opposite message. Now risk-averse pols, already all too aware of the culture-war baggage the gun issue has historically carried, will have no incentive to put their political futures in jeopardy by proposing or supporting gun control legislation. Indeed, it doesn't seem far-fetched to think that gun control might go back into the policy deep-freeze where Democrats had it stowed for most of the last 10 years.

Politicians, to be obvious about it, value survival. They're not inclined to take stands on issues that put them at odds with their constituents, and they don't like to wade into divisive debates that rile people up but don't win them votes. The gay marriage campaigners I wrote about last year understood this extremely well. They spent years developing the credibility to assure politicians that if they voted in favor of gay marriage, advocates would have their back in elections. Marc Solomon, now the national campaign director for Freedom to Marry, ran campaigns for MassEquality a decade ago. The Massachusetts supreme court had just legalized gay marriage, and lawmakers wanted to amend the state constitution to overturn the decision. MassEquality had to convince 75 percent of the legislature, over the course of two legislative sessions, to oppose putting the amendment on the ballot. Only about 25 percent were with him at the beginning. But MassEquality fought to reelect every lawmaker that took its side—in the face of a major statewide Republican campaign backed by then governor Mitt Romney.

"We had two electoral cycles, 2004 and 2006, where we reelected every lawmaker who voted our way," Solomon told me. "Some of these people were not easy to reelect—alcoholism, ethics issues, bad votes. Some didn't collect enough signatures [to get on the ballot] and had to run write-in campaigns. We were determined to reelect every single one. Some

States and Gun Control

While the focus of most of the nation is on Washington, much of what happens with regard to gun control takes place in the 50 states. It is there that we see evidence of the strong differences of opinion regarding how to deal with gun violence and the rights of gun owners. . . .

Despite the legislative failures at the national level, several states passed very strict laws in the wake of the Newtown [Connecticut school] shooting. Most prominent among them were Connecticut, New York, Maryland, and Colorado. At the same time, more than a dozen states loosened gun restrictions, mostly dealing with concealed-carry laws, although Kansas declared that no federal gun laws could be enforced in the state, a law that realistically could not be enforced or pass constitutional muster.

Much of the national focus on state activity centered on Colorado, a western state that had become more urban and more liberal over the past several decades. The state passed several regulations, including comprehensive background checks for private sales and limiting magazine capacity to 15. It was a hard-fought battle that left harsh feelings. Citizen-led recall initiatives placed two key Democratic state legislators on the ballot for recall in special elections. John Morse, the senate president who was instrumental in pushing the laws, and Angela Giron of Pueblo were both defeated in elections that would not typically draw national media attention.

Harry L. Wilson,
The Triumph of the Guns-Right Argument:
Why the Gun Control Debate Is Over.
Santa Barbara, CA: Praeger, 2015.

of those people are now in prison, but we got them reelected."
And Massachusetts politicians learned that if you voted for
gay marriage, you would have a powerful friend and ally.

Fear of the NRA

When it comes to gun control, politicians have feared the
NRA for decades. They've seen Democrats lose at every level,
from president on down, in part because of the gun issue, and
they saw their party make a comeback, particularly out west,
when it started embracing gun rights instead.

The supposedly new-and-improved gun control lobby was
convinced that conventional wisdom was out of date. It set
out to convince politicians that the landscape had changed. It
had a less inflammatory message and more modest goals than
the would-be gun prohibitionists of the 1980s and '90s. It had
a public that seemed galvanized by the shootings in Tucson
[Arizona] and Aurora [Colorado] and Newtown [Connecti-
cut], and polling data that seemed to show voters overwhelmingly supportive of its aims. The NRA's message and tactics,
by contrast, seemed laughably antique and tone-deaf. A vote
for gun control, advocates claimed, wasn't just a safe vote; it
was the only safe vote. Senators who voted against the federal
gun control bill were punished with ad campaigns and saw
their approval ratings dip. For the first time, the terrible calcu-
lus of politics seemed to be on gun control advocates' side.

But there was still one thing they needed to prove. They
needed to prove that they could protect the lawmakers whom
they coaxed out on a limb. On Tuesday, they failed that test.
Future lawmakers facing similar votes aren't going to care
about the particulars; they're going to look at John Morse and
Angela Giron and think, *That's going to be me. No thanks.*

Among gun control campaigners, recriminations are flying
behind the scenes about the strategic missteps that allowed
Tuesday's recalls to slip away. But many are convinced that the
damage will be limited. Matt Bennett, a veteran gun policy

strategist and researcher now with the center-left think tank Third Way, pointed me to a poll that showed that even recall supporters still favored gun background checks; it was Colorado's ban on high-capacity magazines they revolted against.

But panicky lawmakers are unlikely to make such a fine distinction. All they'll see is a fight between Bloomberg's lofty promises and the creaky old tactics of the NRA, and the NRA won.

"I am proud to be a New Yorker because New York is doing something. . . . We are fighting back."

New York Passed Gun Control Legislation Following School Shooting

Kenneth Lovett

Kenneth Lovett is a writer for the New York Daily News. *In the following viewpoint, Lovett reports on sweeping gun control legislation passed in New York State following the 2012 Newtown, Connecticut, school shooting. The gun control package included restrictions on weapons with military features, restrictions on bullets, and background checks for ammunition buyers. The package was passed quickly with the backing of Governor Andrew Cuomo, despite opposition from Republicans and the National Rifle Association of America, who argued that Cuomo was pursuing his presidential ambitions rather than good policy.*

As you read, consider the following questions:

1. Why does Lovett mention the Bushmaster AR-15 in particular as a weapon that the new legislation bans?

2. What did Nicole Malliotakis say should have been the first order of legislative business, rather than gun control?

3. What is one mistake Lovett mentions in the bill that will have to be fixed?

New York on Tuesday [in January 2013] took the lead in the national fight against gun violence when Gov. [Andrew] Cuomo signed into law a sweeping package of gun control measures—including a major expansion of the state's assault weapons ban.

The governor signed the bill just before dinner time, minutes after the [New York State] Assembly sent it to his desk on a 104–43 vote. He called it "the most comprehensive package in the nation."

"I am proud to be a New Yorker because New York is doing something," Cuomo said. "We are fighting back."

The measure sailed through on a fast track, negotiated in the weeks after the Dec. 14 [2012] Newtown, Conn., shooting rampage. It was pushed by Cuomo, who wanted New York to be the first state to tighten its gun laws after the tragedy.

The law took effect immediately—before President [Barack] Obama could announce his own sweeping proposal for action on the federal level to curb gun violence. Obama was set to detail his plan on Wednesday.

The new state law expands the definition of banned weapons to include semiautomatic pistols and rifles with at least one military-style feature. As a result, the Bushmaster AR-15 used in the shooting that killed 20 first graders and six adults at Sandy Hook Elementary School in Newtown would be banned.

New Yorkers who own one of the now-banned weapons can either sell them outside the state or keep them. But if they keep the arms, they have up to a year to register them in a statewide firearms database being created.

The package also bans any gun magazine that can hold more than seven rounds of ammunition, down from the current 10. It requires background checks of ammunition buyers. And ammo dealers will have to register with the state so police can track in real time if someone is stockpiling bullets.

Mayor [Michael] Bloomberg, who has become a national advocate for gun control, praised the Cuomo package as a "big step."

"I think this protects the Second Amendment rights of people and at the same time makes all New Yorkers safer," Bloomberg said.

The National Rifle Association [of America, NRA] denounced the new law and Cuomo, saying the governor was so driven by political ambition that he was "determined to steal the thunder from an anti-gun White House."

"The legislature caved to the political demands of a governor and helped fuel his personal political aspirations," the NRA said. "Such an assault in Albany on Second Amendment rights and democracy is the true assault weapon."

During a grueling five-hour assembly debate Tuesday, many Republicans made similar arguments—while arguing that the new law will not save lives.

"Why are we being bullied into voting on this bill without our proper, responsible due diligence?" said Steve Katz (R-Westchester). "Solely due to the governor's misguided, egotistic notion that this will advance his presidential aspirations."

Even while voting in favor of the bill, Staten Island Assembly Republican Nicole Malliotakis said helping Hurricane Sandy victims, not a gun package, should have been the opening salvo of the new legislative session.

Poll Showing Support for Gun Control in New York State, 2015

	All Voters	Responses Among:		
		Non-gun Household	Gun Household	Gun Owners
Percentage who believe the problem of gun crime and gun violence in New York State is 'extremely' or 'very' serious.	61%	70%	43%	39%
Percentage who agree that: 'The easy availability of guns in the U.S. is a major reason why America has a higher death rate from guns than all other developed nations.'	64%	77%	41%	34%
Percentage who disagree that: 'Having a gun in the home makes the occupants of that home safer.'	52%	65%	24%	22%
Percentage who agree that: 'The public has a right to set reasonable restrictions on the ownership and use of firearms.'	75%	78%	68%	67%
Percentage who believe that: 'Strengthening New York's gun laws will help improve public safety.'	64%	76%	37%	26%

TAKEN FROM: Kiley & Company, "Key Findings from Statewide Voter Survey on Gun Safety," April 29, 2015.

"I lost 22 people in my district in the storm," she said noting that only five people statewide were killed with a rifle.

But Democrats argued the measures will curb the violence.

Cuomo applauded lawmakers—particularly Republicans—for standing up to "extremists"—an apparent reference to the NRA, which had gun owners inundate legislators with calls and e-mails opposing the bill.

But proving just how difficult an issue it was for Republicans, state senate GOP leader Dean Skelos of Long Island was not at the bill signing, even though he helped negotiate the package and voted for it.

Republicans insisted that the final package includes tougher criminal penalties and better ways to keep guns out of the hands of the mentally ill.

And so the new law, known as NY SAFE [Act], for New York Secure Ammunition and Firearms Enforcement Act, seeks to keep guns out of the hands of the mentally ill by requiring health professionals to report to the state if someone is a danger.

That person's name would be added to a database that can be checked periodically when gun licenses are sought or renewed every five years.

The new statute also expands Kendra's Law, which allows judges to order treatment for seriously disturbed individuals.

The package also mandates life without parole for anyone who kills an on-duty first responder—a response to the Christmas Eve shooting murders of two upstate firefighters responding to a blaze set by the killer.

Cuomo told the *Daily News* he hopes the "comprehensive" set of laws can be an example for other states and the federal government.

"I think people tend to look to New York and a New York action resonates," he said. "To the extent this provokes more debate and more action, all the better."

For Cuomo, who is eyeing a potential 2016 presidential run, the tough gun package gives him another signature achievement less than two years after winning passage of a bill to legalize gay marriage.

"It's a big plus in the shadow campaign already being waged for 2016," said University of Virginia political expert Larry Sabato.

The bill moved so fast, some mistakes were made and will have to be corrected in separate legislation in the weeks ahead, lawmakers acknowledge. One problem: Police agencies were not exempted from the restrictions on bullets.

> "We will never be able to prevent all gun violence, but we can certainly do more as a society to prevent the most needless kind—and we can start with simple safety."

Better Gun Safety at Home Can Prevent School Shootings

Richard Aborn

Richard Aborn is the president of the Citizens Crime Commission of New York City. In the following viewpoint, Aborn argues that many school shootings are the result of children getting access to dangerous weapons. He says that better safety measures are needed. These should include better, more comprehensive education; research into why and how children access guns; and laws punishing adults for failure to keep guns from children. Aborn concludes that both gun rights and gun control advocates should be able to agree on better safety measures.

As you read, consider the following questions:

1. What school shooting incidents does Aborn describe to open his viewpoint?

2. What are the circumstances of most shooting deaths in the home, according to Aborn?

3. What are child access prevention laws, and what evidence does Aborn provide that they are effective?

A school shooting that left a teacher in Nevada dead last week [in October 2013] brings the number of such shootings in the United States to 17 since last December's tragedy in Newtown, Conn. Also last week, a Washington State boy was arrested after he brought a gun and 400 rounds of ammunition to his middle school.

Keep Guns from Children

As Americans reflect on these horrifying events, we should also consider how preventable they were. In fact, many of the school shootings this year and in the past could have been prevented with just commonsense safety measures in the home—no new legislation or rules needed.

The gun used in the shooting in Sparks, Nevada—which left the teacher and the shooter, his 12-year-old student, dead and two classmates seriously wounded—was a Ruger 9mm semiautomatic handgun that was apparently taken by the child from his home. While it isn't yet known exactly how he gained access to this dangerous weapon, it is highly likely that serious safety measures were not put in place by the parents, allowing an immature mind to once again wield terrible power.

In the last year, this devastating scenario has played out again and again. School shootings at Sandy Hook Elementary School in Newtown [Connecticut], Red Lake High School in Red Lake, Minn., in 2005, and Heath High School in West Paducah, Ky., in 1997, also involved legal guns taken from the home, used by young people who clearly should not have been able to carry them to school as easily as they would a packed lunch. Sadly, it is perhaps more surprising that these incidents don't occur more regularly. A 2005 study on firearm access in America showed that 1.69 million children under the age of 18 lived in homes with loaded and unlocked firearms.

Newtown, of course, was also made possible by a parent's apparently irresponsible behavior as a gun owner. Although the shooter, 20-year-old Adam Lanza, was not actually school-age when he murdered 26 people at the school, he had easy access to an armory of weapons, even though his own brother questioned Lanza's competence and other relatives described him as "not well."

Illegal guns should be America's No. 1 public safety concern, and new laws are badly needed to eventually curb the violence they allow. But it is unacceptable that legal guns continue to be nearly as deadly as illegal guns when responsible firearm ownership is all that is needed to prevent many of those deaths. Not only are murders like the ones in Newtown and Sparks more likely to happen without better safety measures, but so are accidents: 89 percent of unintentional shooting deaths of children are in the home and usually when children are playing with a loaded gun without their parents present.

To fix this, Americans can take simple steps to block firearm access to children and to prevent the worst kind of carnage.

Better Gun Education Needed

First and foremost, a concerted effort among state governments, firearms dealers, law enforcement, health care workers, and gun manufacturers must be coordinated to ensure that as many gun owners receive basic safety information and warnings about irresponsible firearm storage as possible. Right now, there are various separate attempts at education, which are clearly insufficient. These groups can, and do, disagree mightily about the use and proliferation of guns in this country, but they can all certainly agree that targeted education to prevent so much death is badly needed. Together, under a unified message and strategy, they will be more successful.

Second, Americans must invest in more research to better understand why children use guns against others and how to stop them, including risk factors, incident triggers, and effective interventions. Part of this research must also focus on the increasing links between social media and juvenile violence, and how violent behavior online—such as taunting posts on Facebook and Instagram photos and videos—may interface with devastating real-world consequences.

Finally, there are legislative solutions to pursue as well. "Child access prevention" laws impose specific criminal liability on adults who negligently allow kids to access their firearms. Studies have shown that these laws reduce both unintentional firearm deaths and suicides of children in the states where they are enacted. Twenty-eight states have these laws.

The parents and relatives who have enabled children to use their guns to kill surely feel remorse, and may even face criminal and civil prosecution for their negligence. But Americans, too, should feel responsible when these heart-breaking deaths occur because we have not done enough, as a country, to prevent them.

We will never be able to prevent all gun violence, but we can certainly do more as a society to prevent the most needless kind—and we can start with simple safety.

> *"Because children are naturally curious and impulsive,* and *because we have shown time and again that we cannot 'gun proof' them with education, we have a responsibility to keep guns out of the hands of children."*

Teaching Children Gun Safety Is Not Effective

Marjorie Sanfilippo

Marjorie Sanfilippo is a professor of psychology and associate dean of faculty at Eckerd College in St. Petersburg, Florida. In the following viewpoint, Sanfilippo discusses her research involving children and gun safety. Over several studies, she has found that telling young children to stay away from guns is ineffective, and that children will pick up and point guns at each other even when they have been taught not to do so. She concludes that parents have a responsibility to keep guns away from children, since it is clear that children who find guns will play with them and put themselves and others in danger.

As you read, consider the following questions:

1. Why does Sanfilippo say she agreed to reproduce her research in 1999 for ABC's *20/20* program?

2. How did Sanfilippo make the test scenario more realistic in her second segment for ABC?

3. What does Sanfilippo say should supersede the right to bear arms?

Sadly, some news stories are never old. Twenty years ago, I began my research into children's behavior around firearms, testing the effectiveness of a gun safety program. Hoping to find that the educational initiative would show a positive impact, I was dismayed when four- to six-year-old children played with the disarmed but real handguns. I initially shelved the study; after all, nonsignificant findings are the death knell of academic research. But then I thought about it—isn't it important that people know that programs *don't* work? I wrote it up and published it in an academic journal, dismayed though that the people who *really* need to know about the results—parents—would be unlikely to ever read it.

Children and Unintentional Gun Death

And so it was with that motivation that I said "yes" to the producers of ABC's *20/20* when they asked if I would assist them in recreating my research. The episode, which aired in 1999, generated significant response—both positive and negative. That was the year of the Columbine [High School] shootings, the year that *six* school shootings took place, killing 16 and injuring 35 others. According to the Centers for Disease Control and Prevention [CDC], that was also the year that 467 children ages 1 to 14 lost their lives to gunfire; 88 of these deaths were unintentional and 105 were suicides. The shooters involved in unintentional deaths are almost always children as well.

Fast-forward 15 years. Another phone call, another request from ABC. Would I be willing to assist them again? My first thought was, "Why again?" Children are no less curious and impulsive than they were 15 years ago and guns are no less dangerous. Two studies I had published since 1999 had supported my original findings. In the first, I demonstrated that even a week-long program was ineffective in reducing children's play with handguns; in the second, I demonstrated that guns held a unique allure, qualitatively different from other forbidden objects. In all three studies, more than half of the children played with the guns, and most denied doing so when asked.

Stop! Don't Touch!

As I considered the request from ABC, I realized that here was a chance to reach a new generation of parents and to address the criticisms of the first show, primarily that placing guns in a toy box is confusing to children and that by doing so, children will think the guns are toys. This time, we could do what I had always wanted to do—make the scenario more realistic. So, we conducted the study again, educating the children about the dangers of guns and telling them to get help from an adult if they ever saw one. The children knew what to do—they repeated the mantra again and again. Then, a few days later, we returned, placed a handgun in a backpack in the classroom and rifles on the ground outside. Through the hidden cameras, we watched. Nothing had changed; children still picked up the guns, still peered down the barrel, and still shot each other, and they did so after having said out loud, "Stop! Don't touch! Leave the area! Get an adult!"

Since 1999, when the first show on *20/20* aired, there have been 61 more school shootings (not including those at universities and colleges), resulting in 42 deaths and 86 injuries. The shooters were children, and the guns they used they almost always got from their homes. In 2010 (the most recent year for which the CDC has data), there were 362 firearm-related deaths in children ages 1 to 14; 62 were unintentional and 81 were suicides. Fewer deaths; that's progress, yes, but each of those 362 deaths could have been prevented if parents had taken their responsibilities as seriously as they take their rights.

Rights, but Also Responsibilities

There are always stories behind the numbers. In Sparks, Nev., a 12-year-old boy shot and killed his math teacher and injured two students using a semiautomatic 9mm handgun he took from his parents' home. In Louisville, Ky., a 5-year-old boy shot and killed his 2-year-old sister with a .22 caliber single shot rifle his parents bought him for his birthday. In Tom's River, N.J., a 4-year-old boy shot and killed his 6-year-old friend with a .22 caliber rifle that he found in his home. In Orange County, Texas, a 5-year-old boy shot and killed himself with his babysitter's semiautomatic .40 caliber pistol, which she had left on the coffee table while she napped. In Fayetteville, N.C., a 2-year-old girl shot and killed herself with her father's .22 caliber pistol, which he had left under the couch. In Dundee, Mich., a 3-year-old boy shot and killed himself with a .40 caliber handgun found in a closet in his home.

Hopefully the *20/20* episode prompted some parents to lock up their guns, but in some cases it prompted angry criticism—from gun enthusiasts, NRA [National Rifle Association of America] members, and others who are fearful that "we" are trying to take away their guns, their "rights" under the Constitution. But let me be clear. This is not about the Second Amendment or about a citizen's right to bear arms. This is about the responsibilities that *come* with that right. This is about adults' responsibility to keep children safe. After all, the right of children to live without fear and danger supersedes a constitutional right to bear arms.

We put gates around swimming pools to keep children from drowning. We put safety caps on medications to keep children from poisoning themselves. Like bodies of water and colorful pills, a gun is what the law of torts calls "an attractive nuisance." In other words, guns present a unique allure for children, especially for boys. For that reason, and because children are naturally curious and impulsive, *and* because we have shown time and again that we cannot "gun proof" them with education, we have a responsibility to keep guns out of the hands of children.

Periodical and Internet Sources Bibliography

The following articles have been selected to supplement the diverse views presented in this chapter.

Dewey G. Cornell	"Gun Violence and Mass Shootings—Myths, Facts and Solutions," *Washington Post*, June 11, 2014.
Every Town for Gun Safety	"150 School Shootings in America Since 2013," October 3, 2015.
Ashley Fantz, Lindsey Knight, and Kevin Wang	"A Closer Look: How Many Newtown-Like School Shootings Since Sandy Hook?," CNN, June 19, 2014.
Husna Haq	"Should Public Schools Teach How to Use Guns? Yes, Say South Carolina Legislators," *Christian Science Monitor*, January 8, 2015.
Patrick Lewis	"Gun Safety Would Increase If It Was Taught in Our Schools," *Wyoming Tribune Eagle*, May 7, 2015.
Moms Demand Action and Mayors Against Illegal Guns	"Analysis of School Shootings: December 15, 2012–February 10, 2014," February 12, 2014.
Bob Owens	"Why Aren't We Teaching Firearm Safety in School?," Bearing Arms, July 24, 2014.
Suzi Parker	"Should Public Schools Teach Kids How to Handle Guns?" TakePart, February 20, 2013.
Michele Richinick	"Gun Violence in Schools Among Parents' Main Concerns," MSNBC, August 12, 2014.
Valerie Strauss	"The Alarming Number of School Shootings Since 2012 Killings in Newtown," *Washington Post*, December 10, 2014.

OPPOSING
VIEWPOINTS®
SERIES

CHAPTER 3

Can Security Measures Make Schools Safer?

Chapter Preface

A long-term trend toward more and more complicated security systems in schools has emerged. Security measures often include metal detectors and sometimes even armed guards. They also can include an expanded use of security cameras.

Security camera use increased in particular following the Sandy Hook Elementary School shooting in Newtown, Connecticut, in December 2012. According to Stephen Imbusch, the principal of Walpole High School in Massachusetts, in an *Education Week* article, "Sandy Hook is probably one of the things that has pushed the funding this time around. People are more aware of the need for camera surveillance in schools." Imbusch added that the cameras have helped in determining guilt or innocence in criminal and disciplinary issues. He also thinks they may prevent violence and crime because "when people see a camera, they may be less inclined to do something, so they're preventive."

Similarly, Ben Lang, director of technology at the Novato Unified School District in California, said that most parents in his district saw security cameras as a commonsense measure. "There was very little to almost no pushback in the district, in the community. The community saw it as child safety, an improvement upon child safety and protecting our property against theft and vandalism," he told National Public Radio's Neal Conan in a September 2012 interview.

Once cameras are installed, though, concerns about how they are used and whether they are used to invade student privacy can arise. Conan, for example, notes that at one school, a dean saw two girls kissing in the hallway and shared security footage tape with one of the parents.

The American Civil Liberties Union (ACLU) worries that if school security officers wear body cameras, tapes of students misbehaving, fighting, or engaging in other illegal or embarrassing activity might become a permanent part of their records. Footage of arrests has sometimes gone viral online; that hasn't happened with students, but the fear is that a juvenile infraction could make a student widely recognizable or even unemployable. "Really, what it would become is just a tool for filming and capturing students in their schools," argued Chad Marlow of the ACLU in an *Education Week* article. "It's too much of an infringement on privacy given the other factors at play."

The authors of the viewpoints in the following chapter debate the pros and cons of school safety measures, including metal detectors, armed guards, and zero-tolerance policies.

> *"Is it so crazy to have a police presence in every public school? I say it's worth examining."*

Police in Schools Make Students Safer

Steve Adubato

Steve Adubato is a former New Jersey state legislator, a news anchor, and a Star-Ledger *columnist. In the following viewpoint, Adubato argues that following the school shooting in Newtown, Connecticut, all options to make children safer should be considered. He says that options should include gun control, mental health counseling, and stationing police officers in schools. Adubato says that children are accustomed to seeing armed guards in banks and other areas, and that it should not be hard to explain to children that the guards are there for their protection. He argues against those who oppose police in schools on principle and concludes that any method is worth trying to ensure children's safety.*

As you read, consider the following questions:

1. According to the viewpoint, why does Ceasefire NJ oppose the presence of police in schools?

2. What was the Monmouth County experiment, and how much did it cost, according to Adubato?

3. Besides police in schools, what other solutions to gun violence does Adubato mention at the end of his viewpoint?

The horrific Sandy Hook Elementary School shooting in Newtown, Connecticut [in 2012], which took the lives of 20 children as well as six faculty and staff has raised the inevitable question: How can we protect our children from violence perpetrated by a madman fully armed and intent on mass murder?

For Children's Protection

The more we hear from government officials, advocates on both sides of the gun control issue, and other concerned parties, the more I'm convinced that there is no single solution. Further, I think any measure that has the potential to protect our children is worthy of consideration.

As might be expected, after the Sandy Hook tragedy the National Rifle Association [of America, NRA] suggested placing an armed law enforcement professional in every school. The NRA even advocated arming teachers. That's ludicrous. But is it so crazy to have a police presence in every public school? I say it's worth examining.

Not everyone agrees. "It's just not a solution or even [a means to reduce] the kind of violence that it would be intended to combat," says Nicola Bocour, project director for Ceasefire NJ. "When it comes to dealing with the culture of violence in this country and general concerns over allowing our children to become overly desensitized, having them start from kindergarten and go all the way through high school with military weapons in their face is not the way to go."

I respect the work of Ceasefire NJ, an organization dedicated to reducing gun violence. However, there are armed security guards in banks, department stores, airports and other public places. That's the nature of modern society. We should be able to explain to our children that the armed officer in their school is part of a larger effort to protect them, along with evacuation and disaster drills.

Clearly, there is no reason any private citizen should be able to legally purchase an assault weapon or have a magazine that carries more than 10 bullets. An armed security presence in our schools could be combined with tougher national gun control laws such as the proposals advocated by President Barack Obama as well as our own [New Jersey] Senator Frank Lautenberg.

After the events in Connecticut, the Marlboro Township Board of Education placed a police officer in each of its nine schools for a test period of 90 days. The cost of the Monmouth County town's experiment was approximately $100,000.

Newtown law enforcement officials will eventually file a report on Sandy Hook. Marlboro's mayor, Jonathan Hornik, told my NJTV colleague Mike Schneider on the weeknight news show *NJ Today* that the town will review that before drawing any conclusions. "We will wait to see what comes out, and our police department will make some recommendation to the Board of Ed, and then we will make a decision of whether to continue the police in our schools program."

Look at All Options

To New Jersey's credit, the state has some of the strongest gun control laws in the nation. Governor Chris Christie has made it clear that he doesn't like the idea of armed guards in our schools. "I think that this moment should cause us to foster a national discussion about violence in our society," Christie told me in a televised interview at NJPAC [New Jersey Performing Arts Center]. "And that includes discussing gun control laws, mental health counseling, substance abuse counseling, and violence in media . . . both in television and movies and in video games. All of those things have contributed to a desensitizing of our society to violence."

I agree with the governor that protecting our children from gun violence calls for a multifaceted approach. Rather than focus on a single solution, our approach should be "by any means necessary." We need to do everything we can, but then we have to face the fact that no matter what we do, there is no guarantee we can and will be able to prevent tragedies like Sandy Hook and Columbine [referring to the school shooting at Columbine High School in Colorado in 1999].

That is the toughest reality of all.

So let's put everything on the table. A police presence in our schools. A national ban on assault weapons. Greater restrictions on the number of bullets a magazine can hold. More effective mental health screening of those who would purchase guns.

The time for rigid ideological positions on this complex issue is long past. We need compromise and reasonable discourse. Our children deserve nothing less.

> "Armed security guards may do more
> harm than good to morale inside the
> school."

Armed Guards Will Not Make Schools Safer

Nell Gluckman

Nell Gluckman is a reporter in New York City. In the following viewpoint, Gluckman argues that armed guards in schools will not make students safer. In the event of an armed gunman in a school, there may be little that a guard can do. Further, armed guards often make students feel that school is unsafe and dangerous. Gluckman further maintains that armed guards can sometimes be a threat to students if the guards are not disciplined or if a student manages to get hold of a guard's gun. Guards are also very expensive. Gluckman recommends safety drills as a better way to protect students against threats.

As you read, consider the following questions:

1. What has South Dakota done that Gluckman says will not make schools safer?

2. What safety measures in schools does Gluckman say have been shown to make students feel less safe?

3. What does Gluckman say money for armed guards should be used for instead?

Fourteen years ago [in April 1999], two students at Columbine High School gunned down 13 kids before killing themselves. Forgotten in the maelstrom of the coverage and its aftermath was the fact that the school had an armed guard on duty. He was the first to exchange gunfire with the killers that infamous day. Obviously, it wasn't enough.

Guards Do Not Protect Students

Protecting students from well-armed gunmen who are determined to kill is not as simple as having armed security guards in schools. In fact, armed security guards may do more harm than good to morale inside the school.

Now, in the wake of the tragedy in Newtown, CT, where 26 children and teachers were massacred in its elementary school, South Dakota has become the first state to authorize teachers to carry guns in schools, the *New York Times* reported. This kind of action will not make schools safer.

One middle school principal in Brooklyn believes giving the security guards guns would give "a negative connotation to the building." Principal Barry Kevorkian of Ditmas [Junior High] School says that guns in his building would ratchet up students' fear of a potential intruder. It would make parents feel that he didn't have control of the building.

A study, published in the journal *Youth Society*, supports Kevorkian's view, to some degree. The study found that the presence of certain security measures in schools actually made students feel less safe. Metal detectors and security cameras made all students feel less safe, while the presence of security guards increased only white students' perceptions of fear. The study noted that things like metal detectors and security cam-

Police Brutality in Schools

One afternoon, I was checking my mailbox in the main office of the high school where I worked in the South Bronx. Suddenly, the quiet that settled upon the school late in the day was shattered as three police officers pushed a small black boy through the office door about ten feet from where I stood. A stocky white male officer pinned the boy, who appeared to be no older than thirteen, against the wall. The officer yelled directly into the boy's face and pressed on his chest. The boy was letting out loud sobs, unable to speak. A female officer tried unsuccessfully to ease her colleague away from the student. I stood in shock, unable to respond. The only other person in the room, a Latina school aide in her late fifties—a grandmotherly figure—who had been sitting at one of the desks, slowly and calmly stood up and walked over to the commotion. Stepping between the student and the officer, the woman slipped her arms around the boy and asked him what he needed to do. The officer backed off, and the boy, still sobbing, uttered his first comprehensible words: "I wanna call my mother."

Kathleen Nolan, Police in the Hallways:
Discipline in an Urban High School.
Minneapolis: University of Minnesota Press, 2011.

eras could serve as "cues to danger." They could result in distracting students from learning, increasing levels of disorder and promoting a feeling of mistrust in the school community.

The same study warned school administrators away from quick, costly fixes that don't necessarily solve the problem. The *Washington Post* calculated that placing armed guards in America's schools would cost upward of $2.5 billion a year.

Currently, the New York [City] Police Department [NYPD] assigns safety agents to each of New York City's public schools. These unarmed officers receive the same training as regular police officers, so it might seem a simple step to give them guns in order to ward off potential assailants. However, even trained personnel are not necessarily fit to stop the horrific scenes that have played out in America's schools over the past several decades.

"You can never be prepared for nothing like that," said a safety agent at Ditmas [Junior High] School when asked about school shootings. He did not want his name printed because he said he is not allowed to speak to the press.

Armed Guards May Hurt Students

No matter how prepared, armed guards run the risk of harming the innocent. Last summer nine bystanders were shot by well-trained NYPD police officers who were chasing a gunman in front of the Empire State Building.

Furthermore, some principals don't trust every guard that the police department places in their schools.

"It's really hit or miss in terms of quality and competency," said the principal of an elementary school in lower Manhattan of the safety agents. She said she did not want to be identified because the issue is so controversial. "I worry about a gun being in the wrong hands," she said.

The safety agent at her school had a different worry. He expressed concern over unruly students finding a way to take a gun from an officer.

The Department of Education requires that all schools practice safety drills, which are much more effective in helping students feel proactive about their safety, while still preserving the feeling of security in a school. One of the three kinds of drills that the lower Manhattan elementary school practices is specifically designed to protect students from a gunman in its halls. Teachers lock classroom doors and windows that open out onto the school's central corridor while students hide.

"I'd rather that they have those lessons than think that there's always going to be someone out there to protect them," said the principal.

Let's be honest not only about the cost in morale, but the cost in priorities. Armed guards do not come cheap. The high cost of bringing more guns into campuses could be used instead to enrich the curriculum, hire new classroom teachers and provide mental health services to children.

| "On-campus metal detectors create a
'cycle of disorder.'"

Metal Detectors Do Not Make Schools Safer

Dan Koller

Dan Koller is a reporter at Park Cities People. *In the following viewpoint, Koller reports on experts who have said that metal detectors tend to make students feel less safe, as though they are in a prison-like environment. He also reports that experts argue that metal detectors cannot necessarily keep all guns out of school and that a better method to prevent violence is for teachers to know their students and identify problems early. Metal detectors, he concludes, are expensive and are not all that effective.*

As you read, consider the following questions:

1. According to the viewpoint, what incident made Pam Kripke push her high school to try to get metal detectors?

2. According to Kenneth Trump, what else must be considered beyond the initial cost of the metal detector?

3. What did administrators at Columbine know that could
have helped them prevent the school shooting there,
according to Annette Fuentes?

Although a spate of threats has some Highland Park High
School [near Dallas, Texas] parents clamoring for the in-
stallation of metal detectors, experts say such a move could do
more harm than good.

Metal Detectors Cause Disorder

That's the opinion of Annette Fuentes, who spent two years
researching her 2011 book, *Lockdown High: When the Schoolhouse Becomes a Jailhouse.* The California-based author cited a
study conducted by Matthew Mayer and Peter Leone, who
teach special education at Rutgers University and the University of Maryland, respectively. They found that on-campus
metal detectors create a "cycle of disorder."

"Those schools may actually create the kind of jail-like,
unwelcoming environment that makes kids feel less safe," Fuentes said. "It's counterintuitive, but it makes sense when you
think about creating an environment with these prison-like
conditions. Kids walk around feeling that something bad is
going to happen, that they are under surveillance, and that
they have to be worried. They can't be secure and safe."

Fuentes said there is no definitive count of how many
public schools use metal detectors. Kenneth Trump, who runs
the National School Safety and Security Services consulting
firm based in Cleveland, said the few schools that use them on
a day-to-day basis have a history of weapons-related issues.

"And in those cases, it's largely an effort to plug the dike
and try to deal with a chronic problem," Trump said.

Pam Kripke, whose daughter is a student at Highland Park,
wrote a column about on-campus security last week [in March
2013] for the *Huffington Post* website. The title was "Ammunition Found in Wealthy Dallas High School; Where Are the

Would Metal Detectors Have Prevented Columbine?

Jefferson County School District, of which Columbine [High School, which experienced a school shooting in 1999] is part, created threat-assessment teams that in each school began to identify students who posed potential risks. [Principal Frank] DeAngelis says he has used the process several times successfully.... Columbine devised an emergency response plan, and each semester it practices evacuations and lockdowns.... People always ask him why there are no metal detectors, DeAngelis says, and he poses his own question. "Would metal detectors have stopped [shooters Dylan] Klebold and [Eric] Harris? They would not. When they came on campus, we had a Jefferson [County] police officer who was armed. He exchanged gunfire. They drove into the parking lot. They're not gonna stop at the metal detector and go through. They came in blasting," he says. "A lot of times metal detectors are false security, and the presence of that security system, or the metal detector—is it really gonna stop another school shooting? Not necessarily. And then you look at the practicality of it. A month after the shooting at Columbine, President [Bill] Clinton came to Dakota Ridge High School to address us, and all because of security reasons, all the people had to go through metal detectors. And it was an hour. Do we do that every day with students and make them go through metal detectors? It's still a place to educate students, and do students, and do parents, want a fortress?"

Annette Fuentes, Lockdown High:
When the Schoolhouse Becomes a Jailhouse.
New York: Verso, 2011.

Metal Detectors?" The column debuted Friday, three days after Kripke unsuccessfully pitched a story to *D Magazine* with a suggested title of "Why Highland Park Won't Install Metal Detectors."

In the column, Kripke said she talked to University Park police chief Gary Adams after a box of .22-caliber shells was found in a boys bathroom at the high school on Feb. 27. She said Adams told her metal detectors would be installed within two days. When that didn't happen, she wrote, Adams said he'd provided school administrators with detailed information on how to purchase them.

But Adams told *Park Cities People* that Kripke's account of their conversation was a slight mischaracterization.

"I told her that I felt like, at that time, the threat was elevated," Adams said, "and it might be a good idea to have metal detectors, that I had worked on trying to locate some metal detectors for that Monday. We have some wands, and we used to have a portable magnetometer. I was looking for some portable magnetometers."

Adams said he was not able to find any on short notice; he advised HPISD [Highland Park Independent School District] superintendent Dawson Orr's staff to search for some on the Internet.

"You can't just magically install magnetometers or walk-through metal detectors in a school overnight," Adams said. "But we have the wands. The school, as a matter of fact, bought wands."

HPISD spokeswoman Helen Williams confirmed that. She also said principal Walter Kelly declined to tell *The Bagpipe*, the high school newspaper, how often the wands are being used.

Teacher Knowledge, Not Metal Detectors

As for airport-style walk-through metal detectors, the website for Garland-based Garrett Metal Detectors lists four models.

Their suggested retail prices range from $4,500 to $5,500. But Trump said there is much more to consider than the initial cost.

"It sounds good, it feels good, but when you start talking about how you implement it," Trump said, "are you going to run it 24/7? Are you going to scan everybody? How are you going to staff it? Are you going to be able to have people guard every other entrance in the building while you're scanning in one? How do you prevent somebody from coming in the night before, dropping stuff off, and then coming in clean?"

Fuentes said metal detectors would have done nothing to prevent the tragedies at Columbine High in Littleton, Colo., and Sandy Hook Elementary in Newtown, Conn. "A metal detector doesn't keep out someone who is determined to get in the school," she said. "If someone is carrying a gun, they're not going to present it at the metal detector for inspection. So it doesn't even bear up under scrutiny as a sensible, logical strategy. But it makes people feel safer."

Fuentes said a better alternative to a "jail-like environment" is making sure that administrators and faculty are familiar with the students in their school. That way, potential issues can be dealt with.

"At Columbine, it was well known, for a long time, that these two young men had serious problems," Fuentes said. "The principal and teachers knew that they were making violent videos that celebrated guns; they were talking about doing damage to other students. These things were discussed, and they were ignored."

Trump said the No. 1 way to find out about weapons in schools is from kids who come forward to tell an adult that they trust. This week's increase of the HPISD reward to $30,000—thanks to an anonymous donation of $20,000—may help in that regard. But Trump also touted the benefits of awareness.

"The first and best line of defense is always a well-trained and highly alert staff and student body," he said, "but that just doesn't give the guarantee that people want."

> "Alisha Mendez, now a high school se-
> nior in Middletown, Pa., said her thirst
> for attention, which turned her into a
> middle school bully, would have been
> quenched faster if her school had had a
> tough anti-bullying policy and enforced
> it."

Zero-Tolerance Policies Can Prevent Bullying

Jim DuBreuil, Cleopatra Andreadis, and Denise Martinez-Ramundo

Jim DuBreuil and Cleopatra Andreadis are producers and De-
nise Martinez-Ramundo is a reporter at ABC News. In the fol-
lowing viewpoint, they argue that bullying in school could be
prevented with education and tough, zero-tolerance anti-bullying
policies. Bullies, they say, enjoy the sense of power and may not
have learned how to empathize with their victims. Teaching chil-
dren that bullying is wrong, and setting up strict consequences,
could end bullying, the authors conclude.

As you read, consider the following questions:

1. According to the viewpoint, what does Alex Whirledge say would have stopped him from bullying?

2. According to the authors, why does Alisha Mendez say she bullied others?

3. What do bullies have in common, according to Dr. Gail Saltz, and what do they not necessarily have in common?

Kids become bullies for myriad reasons, but it seems as if a single force could have stopped them: zero tolerance for bullying in school.

No Tolerance for Bullies

"If that would have happened, zero tolerance, I would think, I would get sent . . . home, get everything taken away from me," said Alex Whirledge of Anaheim, Calif., who was an eighth-grade bully. "It would have stopped."

Alisha Mendez, now a high school senior in Middletown, Pa., said her thirst for attention, which turned her into a middle school bully, would have been quenched faster if her school had had a tough anti-bullying policy and enforced it.

"It would have—180, right around," Mendez told *20/20* coanchor Chris Cuomo.

To date, 45 states have passed laws requiring a range of anti-bullying actions, from implementing prevention programs to reporting incidents to the police. But child behavioral experts say few schools have zero-tolerance policies in place.

"The school needs to be clear about what the ramifications will be for bullying, which most schools are not," said Dr. Gail Saltz, a psychiatrist and author of books about adolescents' thinking.

"There's going to be a price to pay. It's going to be suspension, it's going to be detention, it's going to be something that not only you don't want but your parent [too]."

What drives someone to become a bully in the first place?

"I was a bully because I was being bullied," said Whirledge, now 14 and a high school freshman who plays on the football team.

As a seventh grader, Alex was subjected to the taunting and pushing that seems to be commonplace in schools throughout the United States. Then, in eighth grade, the roles changed. Alex was no longer the victim but the aggressor.

"It felt great," said Alex, adding that being a bully gave him a sense of strength and leadership.

"You taste that powerful feeling of being the one in control. It's very exciting," Saltz explained. "And you can really lose your moral compass."

Alex and his friends were involved in multiple bullying incidents that were never brought to the attention of school officials, mainly because the student victims were afraid of reprisals.

Lunchroom Is Bully Central

Then, in January, the bullied students told the principal. The boys were set to be expelled, but they were suspended instead and put in a mandatory six-week group counseling intervention program. There was no official anti-bullying program in place, but the boys were required to create an anti-bullying presentation as part of the intervention. Alex said it gave him a chance to reflect on the cycle of violence and the best way to prevent it.

"It's a bullying cycle. You want to get revenge, and that's why we created the program to stop the bullying before it starts," said Alex.

Alisha, who spent time in foster care, said she wanted to take out her anger on others.

"I would tease kids in class, in the hallways. I was more of a mental bully instead of a physical bully," Alisha told ABC News. "If somebody would actually try to get smart back with me, I would probably take it to a fighting level."

The crudest room in the school was the lunchroom. "That's where . . . kids bully people. There's the cool kids, the smart kids, the weird kids and everyone sits at different tables and bust on each other, which is slang for make fun. How you acted really was defining if you were gonna get picked on or not," she said.

Ultimately, Alisha decided to reform her ways. She said she hoped a nicer Alisha could serve as a role model for her younger sister and brother.

Saltz said bullies come in all shapes and sizes, but a common thread is that they haven't been taught empathy.

"You know, kids who aren't getting a message that being good and kind and empathetic count, hugely," Saltz said.

"Many kids who are bullying today are actually quite confident. They are athletes, they are attractive, they are academically high performers," Saltz said. "It's not as simple as this dynamic of, you know, I'm failing so I need to get more so I take it out on somebody else."

Making It Uncool to Be a Bully

As with bullies, bullying takes many forms. "A lot of kids don't understand, for instance, that being shunned and left out, although not overtly tortured, is bullying," Saltz said.

Along with strict anti-bullying policies, education is the best approach to end the behavior, she said.

"A lot of it has to do with education, changing the culture. It's not cool to be a bully," Saltz said. "We're not gonna let it happen."

"The research findings and other data on zero tolerance suggest that these policies—which have been in force for 25 years—have no real benefit and significant adverse effects."

Zero-Tolerance Policies Do Not Make Schools Safer

Jacob Kang-Brown et al.

Jacob Kang-Brown is a research associate at the Center on Sentencing and Corrections at the Vera Institute of Justice. In the following viewpoint, he and his coauthors discuss zero-tolerance policies, which are supposed to mandate expulsion or suspension for students who bring a weapon to school. In fact, the authors argue, zero-tolerance policies are often used to expel students for minor disciplinary issues. There is no evidence, they say, that zero-tolerance policies make students safer. Instead, the policies are used disproportionately against black children and other minority students and have a negative effect on their graduation rates and success after school. Given that the policies have no

Jacob Kang-Brown et al., "A Generation Later: What We've Learned About Zero Tolerance in Schools," Center on Youth Justice, December 2013. www.vera.org. Copyright © 2013 Vera Institute of Justice. All rights reserved. Reproduced with permission.

demonstrated benefits and are applied unequally against vulnerable children, the authors recommend discontinuing zero tolerance.

As you read, consider the following questions:

1. According to the viewpoint, what was mandated in the Gun-Free Schools Act of 1994?

2. How much did the rate of high school suspension and expulsion increase between 1972–1973 and 2009–2010, according to the authors?

3. What surprising relationship do the authors discuss between misconduct in school and academic achievement?

In considering different strategies for promoting productive and safe school environments, it can be difficult to know what works and what doesn't. In particular, long-standing debates about zero-tolerance policies leave many people confused about the basic facts. How do these policies that mandate specific and harsh punishments affect individual students and the overall school environment? Have zero-tolerance policies helped to create a school-to-prison pipeline as many people argue? And if the costs outweigh the benefits, are there alternatives to zero tolerance that are more effective?

This [viewpoint] aims to answer these questions by drawing on the best empirical research produced to date, and to identify the questions that remain unanswered. Most importantly, this [viewpoint] strives to be practical. We believe that with a clearer understanding of the facts, policy makers and school administrators can join with teachers and concerned parents to maintain order and safety in ways that enhance education and benefit the public interest.

The Rise of Zero-Tolerance Policies

The culture of discipline in educational settings has changed profoundly over the past 25 years. Disciplinary systems today are much more formal—in many cases, rigid—and severe punishments are applied more broadly, affecting more students. Instead of principals and other school administrators dealing with misconduct on a case-by-case basis, considering the circumstances of the event, the specific students involved, and the repercussions for the overall safety of the school environment, many school districts now have zero-tolerance policies that greatly limit discretion in individual cases, involve law enforcement personnel, and mandate removing students from school. These policies generally require out-of-school suspension or expulsion on the first offense for a variety of behaviors—initially instituted for possession of a weapon or illegal drugs, but now frequently also including smoking tobacco or fighting in school.

The changes began in the late 1980s and quickly gained momentum, fueled in large part by rising rates of juvenile arrests for violent crimes and a climate in which young people were increasingly seen as dangerous. Feeling pressure to do something, Congress applied the rhetoric and intention of tough-on-crime laws to the school environment and passed the Gun-Free Schools Act in 1994.

As a result, to qualify for federal education funds, states had to pass a law requiring all local school districts to expel any student, for at least one year, who brings a weapon to school.

Although the juvenile crime rate peaked in 1994 and declined steadily over the next decade, the idea that young people should be feared stuck. In 1996, political scientist John Dilulio predicted a coming wave of young "super-predators." Following the massacre in 1999 at Columbine High School, people across the country worried that the next devastating school shooting would occur in their town. This is the climate in which zero-tolerance policies proliferated and also expanded to encompass a wide range of misconduct much less harmful than bringing a weapon to school. As early as the 1996–97 school year, 79 percent of schools had adopted zero-tolerance policies for violence, going beyond federal mandates. To put some muscle behind these policies, the federal government and states began to increase funding for security guards and other school-based law enforcement officers and later to install metal detectors. Between the 1996–97 and 2007–08 school years, the number of public high schools with full-time law enforcement and security guards tripled. This shift in school disciplinary policy and practice mirrored changes in the juvenile justice system to make it more closely resemble the adult system.

Suspend and Expel

The most obvious result of the rise in zero-tolerance policies is well documented: The use of out-of-school suspension and expulsion increased almost everywhere and dramatically so in some places. Nationally, the number of secondary school students suspended or expelled over the course of a school year increased roughly 40 percent from one in 13 in 1972–73 to one in nine in 2009–10. In recent years, an estimated two million students annually are suspended from secondary schools. As a point of comparison, slightly more than three million students graduated high school in 2013.

A rigorous and detailed study of students in Texas published in 2011 by the Council of State Governments and the Public Policy Research Institute at Texas A&M University shows how the culture of zero tolerance became so pervasive in that state that harsh punishments are meted out even when they are not strictly required. Researchers tracked every student who entered seventh grade in 2000, 2001, and 2002 for six years. They found that more than half (60 percent) were suspended or expelled at some point in middle or high school. Moreover, the majority of those suspensions and expulsions appear to be for offenses that did not involve behaviors that fell within the parameters of the state of Texas's zero-tolerance mandate; instead, they were simple violations of the schools' codes of conduct, such as using tobacco or acting out in ways that teachers find to be disruptive. In other words, school administrators chose to use harsh punishments even when they had the discretion to do otherwise.

It is important to keep in mind that both national and statewide statistics on school discipline mask wide variation among schools. In the Texas study, for example, even similar schools with similar student populations varied widely in the proportion of students that were suspended or expelled. Some researchers argue that there is now more variation in both the content and implementation of zero-tolerance policies, with some schools punishing both major and minor misconduct harshly while others define and practice zero tolerance as a system of graduated sanctions in which the severity of the punishment matches the seriousness of the offense.

Harsher on Some Students than Others

There is abundant evidence that zero-tolerance policies disproportionately affect youth of color. Nationally, black and Latino students are suspended and expelled at much higher rates than white students. Among middle school students, black youth are suspended nearly four times more often than white youth, and Latino youth are roughly twice as likely to be suspended or expelled than white youth. And because boys are twice as likely as girls to receive these punishments, the proportion of black and Latino boys who are suspended or expelled is especially large. Nationally, nearly a third (31 percent) of black boys in middle school were suspended at least once during the 2009–10 school year. Part of this dynamic is that under-resourced urban schools with higher populations of black and Latino students are generally more likely to respond harshly to misbehavior.

The study in Texas echoes these national statistics and also provides important evidence of an actual inequity in how schools apply these punishments. After controlling for more than 80 individual and school characteristics normally associated with poor academic performance, as well as differences in rates of delinquency and more serious offending, researchers found that black youth were more likely to be disciplined and more likely to receive harsh discipline (such as out-of-school suspension) when those punishments were discretionary.

Race is not the only factor associated with an increased likelihood of being suspended or expelled. Students with special education needs are also suspended or expelled at higher rates. Annually, high school students with disabilities of any sort are nearly three times more likely to receive an out-of-school suspension compared to high school students without disabilities (20 percent versus 7 percent). In the Texas study where almost 60 percent of students were suspended or expelled at least once, the rate among students with educational disabilities reached nearly 75 percent. Rates were highest among students with learning disabilities and emotional disturbances.

Zero-Tolerance Policies Don't Make Schools More Orderly or Safe

Effective discipline plays an important role in schools. It helps to maintain an environment that is conducive to learning by minimizing disruption in the classroom and by fostering the kind of order and predictability that young people need to feel comfortable and remain open to new information and experiences. Discipline can also make a school environment safer for everyone by preventing potentially dangerous, or even deadly, events.

The theory underlying zero-tolerance policies is that schools benefit in both ways when problem students are removed from the school setting. However, there is no research actually demonstrating this effect. No studies show that an increase in out-of-school suspension and expulsion reduces disruption in the classroom and some evidence suggests the opposite effect. In general, rates of suspension and expulsion appear unrelated to overall school success for schools with similar characteristics, levels of funding, and student populations.

Although zero-tolerance policies were created to respond to students caught with a weapon, only five percent of serious disciplinary actions nationally in recent years involve possession of a weapon. In some states the proportion is even lower. In Maryland, for example, less than two percent of suspensions and expulsions are related to carrying a weapon in school, and in Colorado, it is less than one percent. In contrast, nationally 43 percent of expulsions and out-of-school suspensions lasting a week or longer were for insubordination.

While some people would argue that these statistics are evidence of the deterrent effect of zero tolerance, there is no research demonstrating that the threat of harsh punishment actually discourages students from bringing a weapon to school. In addition, survey data collected by the Centers for Disease Control and Prevention show just a modest decline in the proportion of students who claim to have brought a weapon to school in the previous 30 days: 17 percent in 2011, down from 22 percent in 1993.

What the research does show is that over the past two decades, youth crime has become less serious and violent. In fact, the increase in out-of-school suspensions and expulsions occurred at a time when, nationally, rates of serious violent crime among juveniles were falling to the point where they are now the lowest that they've been in decades. At the state level, we see similar, and sometimes more dramatic, patterns: In Colorado, where less than one percent of serious disciplinary actions involve possession of a weapon, the overall number of juvenile arrests has been declining since 1991, and is about 70 percent lower today compared to the early 1990s. The situation in California is similar: The number of felony arrests of juveniles is about 61 percent lower than it was in 1991, and the overall number of youth arrested is at an all-time low.

From Suspension to Disengagement

Some of the most rigorous research conducted on the subject of zero tolerance shows that out-of-school suspension can severely disrupt a student's academic progress in ways that have lasting negative consequences. For similar students attending similar schools, a single suspension or expulsion doubles the risk that a student will repeat a grade. Being retained a grade, especially while in middle or high school, is one of the strongest predictors of dropping out. In one national longitudinal study, youth with a prior suspension were 68 percent more likely to drop out of school.

The long-term effects of failing to complete high school are well documented. Individuals without a high school education have much less earning power and are more likely to be unemployed. In 2012, for example, median earnings among workers nationally was $815 per week, while those without a high school degree earned just $471 per week. And unemployment rates were roughly double: 6.8 percent nationally and 12.4 percent among people who had not completed high school.

Research has revealed an unexpected relationship between misconduct in school and academic achievement. One longitudinal study showed that, while being disconnected from school as a result of student misconduct adversely affects academic achievement, misconduct itself is not directly associated with lower academic achievement. In other words, the misconduct alone does not necessarily lead to poor academic performance. The finding suggests the importance of keeping young people engaged in school, even when, and maybe especially when, they are having behavioral problems.

Suspension Does Not Reduce Violence

When teachers fear the loss of control and the school uses heightened zero-tolerance policies, power struggles increase and result in more classroom disruptions and suspensions. It is a vicious cycle. In a ... study, [Frances] Vavrus and [KimMarie] Cole (2002) examined the social and cultural factors that influence teachers to make the decision to kick students out of class. The school had a large minority enrollment and stressed zero tolerance of violence policies. Two freshman high school science classrooms were studied to find out how disciplinary moments were negotiated. Disciplinary moments are classroom interactions that lead up to, occur before, or prevent exclusionary school discipline. Video-recorded observations, teacher and student interviews, and notes were analyzed.

Vavrus and Cole (2002) found that disciplinary moments varied in each classroom. Decisions made depended on how the teacher and students acted and reacted to each other minute by minute. Disciplinary moments were not the textbook-like series of events that are strictly defined in school discipline policy that presumes a link to violence. Instead, teachers often suspended students from class for unwritten or unspoken violations of classroom conduct codes after multiple disciplinary moments. They usually singled out and sent particular students out of the room when they felt a loss of control. This process did not usually link to violent behavior.

Debra M. Pane and Tonette S. Rocco,
Transforming the School-to-Prison Pipeline: Lessons from the Classroom. *Rotterdam, The Netherlands: Sense Publishers, 2014.*

Is the School-to-Prison Pipeline Real?

Out-of-school suspension is strongly associated with subsequent involvement in the juvenile justice system. The best evidence of this pathway comes from the Texas study, in which a single suspension or expulsion for a discretionary offense that did not include a weapon almost tripled a student's likelihood of becoming involved in the juvenile justice system in the following academic year. The longer-term effects, however, are unclear. While researchers at the Vera Institute of Justice attempted to study this issue, our findings were inconclusive. We still don't know if exposure to harsh discipline in middle or high school—in particular suspension and/or expulsion— increases a person's likelihood of spending time in prison as an adult. We also do not know what effect simply attending a school that practices zero tolerance has on students in the long term, regardless of whether they are suspended or expelled.

While questions linger about the effects of zero tolerance on long-term criminal justice involvement, there is research demonstrating the importance of staying in school: Additional years of compulsory education do help to prevent young people from engaging in delinquency and crime. In addition, there is some evidence that a positive school climate not only lowers overall levels of violence in school, but may also have some beneficial effect on the behavior of young people outside of school, although the relationship is neither simple nor clear.

The Tide Has Turned

Taken together, the research findings and other data on zero tolerance suggest that these policies—which have been in force for 25 years—have no real benefit and significant adverse effects. In August 2013 in a speech before members of the American Bar Association, U.S. Attorney General Eric Holder talked about the need to confront zero-tolerance policies that "do not promote safety" and called on those assembled to remember that educational institutions should be "doorways of opportunity." "A minor school disciplinary offense should put a student in the principal's office and not a police precinct," the attorney general said. Both the American Academy of Pediatrics and the American Psychological Association have issued statements effectively condemning zero-tolerance policies, given their harmful effects, and called instead for students to be disciplined on a case-by-case basis and in a developmentally appropriate manner. Clearly, youth advocates are no longer the lone or loudest voices for change. The tide is turning and it has been for some time.

There's growing consensus that the most effective schools reinforce positive behavior and respond to behavioral problems on a case-by-case basis in ways that suit the individual's circumstances and needs. That implies a return to discretion, but with some structure and guidance. There's still not much research to support this approach, but a recent study showed that positive behavioral support in the classroom is associated with greater order and discipline, fairness, and productive student-teacher relationships, while exclusionary disciplinary strategies (i.e., out-of-school suspension and expulsion) are associated with more disorder overall. In July 2011, the U.S. Department of Justice and the U.S Department of Education announced the creation of the Supportive School Discipline Initiative, which seeks to "promote positive disciplinary options to both keep children in school and improve the climate for learning," among other goals.

Across the country, state departments of education and municipal school districts are moving away from zero-tolerance policies. In 2012, legislators in Colorado revised the state law governing school discipline to encourage school districts to rely less on suspension and expulsion and also mandated and funded additional training for police officers that serve as school resource officers (SROs). While not every school district has revised its code of conduct, and SROs will not receive the mandated training until 2014, the state has already observed the impact with a 27 percent drop in expulsions and 10 percent decrease in suspensions statewide compared with the previous year.

Two years earlier, in 2010, the Boston public school system revised its code of discipline—renaming it a code of conduct—and also implemented restorative justice practices as alternatives to suspension and expulsion. As a result, the number of students suspended or expelled dropped from 743 to 120 in just two years. Officials in Buffalo, New York, made significant changes to the school code for the 2013–14 school year, expanding their commitment to keeping students in school through a system of prevention, intervention, and promoting positive behavior, including both positive behavioral interventions and supports, or PBIS for short, and restorative practices. And in California, where "willful defiance" accounted for nearly half (48 percent) of the more than 700,000 suspensions statewide in 2011–12, the Los Angeles Unified School District Board banned willful defiance as a reason for suspension or expulsion.

We do not know all of the effects of a generation of zero-tolerance policies in our nation's schools, but there is enough information to compel a move away from these practices. Certain facts are clear: Zero tolerance does not make schools more orderly or safe—in fact the opposite may be true. And policies that push students out of school can have lifelong negative effects, perhaps severely limiting a young person's future potential. That is troubling on an individual level for every boy and girl affected and of grave public concern when school systems exclude a significant proportion of the student body, as is the case in more than 300 districts nationwide that suspend and expel more than one in four of their secondary students. Similarly, while we don't fully understand the potential benefits of taking a very different approach to maintaining order and safety in schools, there is a growing body of experience that education administrators and school principals can draw on to inspire and guide their local reform efforts, and that researchers can use to add to the field of "what works."

Periodical and Internet Sources Bibliography

The following articles have been selected to supplement the diverse views presented in this chapter.

Sheila A. Bedi	"We Can't Arrest Our Way to Safer Schools," *U.S. News & World Report*, December 14, 2013.
Allie Bidwell	"How Schools Are Working to Prevent School Shootings," *U.S. News & World Report*, January 15, 2014.
Evid Blad	"Body Cameras on School Police Spark Student Privacy Concerns," *Education Week*, March 4, 2015.
Noah R. Bombard	"Keeping Schools Safe: Are Metal Detectors the Answer for School Safety?," MassLive, May 13, 2015.
Emily DeRuy	"Violence in Schools Is Down. So Why Are We Spending More on Security?," Fusion, May 21, 2015.
James Alan Fox	"Make School Security Invisible," *USA Today*, December 8, 2014.
Elaine Haskins	"Security Screening Detectors Improve School Safety," *Courier Express* (DuBois, PA), May 21, 2015.
Alyssa Morones	"Surveillance Cameras Gain Ground in Schools," *Education Week*, June 5, 2013.
Libby Nelson	"7 in 10 Schools Now Have Shooting Drills, Needlessly Traumatizing Huge Numbers of Children," Vox, May 22, 2015.
Amanda Paulson	"School Discipline: New US Guidelines Shift Away from Zero-Tolerance Policies," *Christian Science Monitor*, January 8, 2014.

OPPOSING
VIEWPOINTS®
SERIES

CHAPTER 4

What Is the Relationship Between Health Care Issues and Student Safety?

Chapter Preface

Lead exposure can cause serious health problems, especially in young children. When lead is inhaled or swallowed (as when small children eat paint chips) it can be distributed throughout the body, damaging red blood cells and preventing bones from absorbing calcium. Lead can also harm the brain, resulting in speech and language problems.

Lead had been a common component in paint because it sped up drying and increased durability. Lobbying efforts by paint companies kept lead in circulation until 1978, when it was finally banned. Although lead paint is no longer in use, many schools and day care centers were painted with lead-based paints that are now chipping. There is little government effort to remove lead paint from schools; no government agency is directly responsible for lead-abatement efforts, and money for lead abatement has been cut drastically in recent years because of the economic downturn and its ongoing effects. This is especially disturbing because, according to Howard Mielke, an expert in lead poisoning at Tulane University, "there is no safe level of exposure" to lead.

Funding cuts for lead abatement are also unfortunate because substantial evidence suggests that lead exposure causes long-term, costly health and behavior problems. Spending on lead cleanup can be expensive, but it is believed to return from $17 to $221 for every dollar spent.

This is because lead's long-term effects are pervasive. For example, a study analyzing data from Milwaukee Public Schools showed that young children exposed to lead were almost three times as likely to be suspended from school by the fourth grade. Lead could therefore be part of the cause of higher rates of discipline problems among African American students, since black children often live in poorer housing with higher amounts of lead. Paul Biedrzycki, director of disease control and environmental health with the City of Milwaukee Health Department, said in an August 2013 article in the *Milwaukee-Wisconsin Journal Sentinel,* that "this study adds to the body of evidence. You can no longer discount low-level lead as not contributing to lower achievement and delinquency, and even criminal behavior down the road." Lead abatement is not just an issue for school health, then, but touches on wide-ranging social problems both within and beyond the school community.

The following chapter examines other school health problems, including mental health issues, bullying, and vaccination.

> "We just have to become much more
> vigilant."

Addressing Mental Illness Can Reduce School Shootings

Rita Price

Rita Price is a reporter for the Columbus Dispatch. *In the following viewpoint, Price reports that depression and mental illness often go unreported among high school students. Students who have mental health issues often do not get help, and their problems may not be recognized by parents or teachers. This can lead to isolation and may be a factor in those students who are involved in school violence. Price concludes that better mental health services and more vigilance are necessary to stop school shootings.*

As you read, consider the following questions:

1. What characteristics are often shared by school shooters, according to Katherine Newman?

2. What does Bernadette Melnyk suggest needs to change in mental health care?

3. What prevents high school teachers from comparing notes about students, according to Janie Bailey?

The Sandy Hook Elementary School shootings in Connecticut [in December 2012] quickly pushed the nation into a bitter conversation about the availability of weapons that, in an instant, can mow down a classroom of 6- and 7-year-olds.

More Children Need Treatment

But gun control is only one part of the post-tragedy analysis. A sociologist who studies school shootings says that, although there is no way to stop all such attacks, the avenues of prevention should cut more deeply through schools, families, the mental health system and the small-town and suburban communities where most school shootings occur.

In the 2004 book *Rampage: The Social Roots of School Shootings*, coauthor Katherine Newman and a team of researchers examined 18 school shootings since 1970 and found that the pictures that emerged bore more than a slight resemblance. Since publication, at least five more mass shootings have occurred in U.S. schools and universities.

Newman, a dean at Johns Hopkins University in Baltimore, said those who became killers were usually first misfits, often scrawny and less physically mature than most of the peers with whom they compete for attention.

They're rarely loners by choice. "Their experience is not one of being alone," Newman said. "It's one of being rejected."

That painful isolation stands out all the more in a small, highly connected community with a lot of "intertwining social capital," she said. Such places are great for people who are able to tap into the tightly knit fabric. "But if you are a marginal person, this is a life sentence of exclusion," Newman said.

And before their lethal attacks, many of the school shooters exhibited warning signs or made threats. Sometimes, other

Men, Mental Health, School Violence

The shootings in Aurora [Colorado], Tucson [Arizona], Virginia Tech, and other massacres ... dramatize the need for better mental health care. The shooters were all males in these examples, yet there appears to be a conspiracy of silence on the issue of men and depression, and mental health care for men is stigmatized in many communities. Addressing the issue of societal gun violence, we need to acknowledge that men with serious mental health issues are the perpetrators of most mass rampage murders and that better mental health care is part of the solution. While the shooters in the massacres mentioned above had been under observation from various mental health facilities, all fell under the radar, amassed loads of weapons, and went on gun rampages, highlighting the need for improved mental health care and better family, community, and school responsibilities for disturbed men. But we also need to address issues of cultures of male violence and crises of masculinity as part of the problem of guns and violence in the contemporary moment.

Douglas Kellner, "School Shootings, Crises of Masculinities,
and Media Spectacle: Some Critical Perspectives."
School Shootings: Mediatized Violence in a Global Age.
Ed. Glenn W. Muschert and Johanna Sumiala.
Bingley, UK: Emerald Group Publishing, 2012.

teens goaded them, Newman said. "The peers realize that they've got someone who can be manipulated. They're pushing his buttons."

She and other experts stressed that they aren't applying this profile to 20-year-old Adam Lanza, the Newtown, Conn., shooter whose life experiences and psychological state remain murky. But when more is known about him, those findings should be reviewed from a broader sociological standpoint, they say.

"We have to do something more than we're doing right now," said Bernadette Melnyk, nursing college dean and chief wellness officer at Ohio State University. "Each time a tragedy like this happens, there is always intense national attention and calls for action. But unfortunately, when the emotion wears off, then no real action is taken to prevent the same type of nightmare from occurring over and over again."

Melnyk recently served on the U.S. Preventive Services Task Force, which recommends primary care screening for depression in children 12 to 18. She said physical and mental health care need to be integrated so that more nurse practitioners and doctors are "dually prepared" to recognize problems.

She said 1 in 4 children and teens has a mental health issue at some point, but less than 25 percent get treatment.

"We do know that other teens and young adults who were involved in other shootings were dealing with mental illness," Melnyk said. "The mental health piece is being missed in so many places."

The stigma of seeking help, lag times between referral and treatment, cost and limited services often are barriers.

More Vigilant

Janie Bailey, CEO [chief executive officer] of Columbus Area, Inc., said the mental health and substance abuse agency is trying to increase services for young people. "Those are the ones we should not look away from," Bailey said. "When we leave them isolated, what are they doing?" Newman said her research found that people often are reluctant to intervene or report disturbing signs. Even a psychiatric nurse whose daughter was killed in the 1998 Jonesboro, Ark., school shooting hadn't gone to authorities when her daughter told her that one of the boys had been shooting cats.

"She just drove her daughter to school and didn't report anything," Newman said. Records and observations about troubled younger students don't make the transition to high school, so slates are wiped clean, Newman said. High school teachers see students for less than an hour a day and might not compare notes with other teachers.

"There are all kinds of professional prohibitions about sharing information," Newman said, adding that the privacy protections are well intentioned. But the result is that there's not a complete picture of the troubled young person.

Newman said community members are not to blame when a potential killer blooms in their midst.

"We just have to become much more vigilant," Bailey said. "We know enough now to say that we really do need to be watching out."

> *"Mental illness is easy to blame, easy to pinpoint, and easy to legislate against in regard to gun ownership. But that doesn't mean that it is the right place to start in an attempt to curtail violence."*

Addressing Mental Illness Is Not a Good Way to Prevent School Shootings

Maria Konnikova

Maria Konnikova is a writer for the New Yorker. *In the following viewpoint, Konnikova reports on research showing that mental illness is a poor predictor of violence. Being male, abusing drugs, and being poor are all better predictors of violence than mental illness, and many school shooters have no real history of mental illness. The best predictor of violence is in fact not mental illness but past violence. Given this, Konnikova concludes, it would be better to focus on risk factors other than mental illness in trying to prevent school shootings.*

As you read, consider the following questions:

1. What surveys does Konnikova cite to show that people link mental illness and violence?

2. What two myths about mental illness and violence does Jeffrey Swanson say his study debunked?

3. What one kind of gun violence was increased by mental illness, according to Swanson's research?

On Friday, October 24th [2014], during the busy lunch hour in the school cafeteria of Marysville-Pilchuck High School, in Marysville, Washington, Jaylen Fryberg opened fire on his classmates, killing one student and wounding four others, three of whom later died from their injuries. Then he killed himself.

Just a week earlier, Fryberg had been crowned prince of the school's homecoming court—he was a community volunteer, student athlete, and all-around "good kid." But within hours of the shooting, that picture had changed. Quickly, media outlets analyzed his tweets, Facebook page, Instagram account, and his text and Facebook messages. He was "full of angst" and "anguished." One media report concluded that "he just wasn't in the right state of mind." Another went further: he was a "depressed sociopath." Many writers pointed out that the Marysville school district had recently received a large federal grant to improve mental health services for students. "We used to have a much greater social safety net," the district supervisor Jerry Jenkins told the *Seattle Times*. "Yes, he was popular, but there came a time when something changed. If people are educated to look for those, these are things they can do [to] intervene," Carolyn Reinach Wolf, a mental health lawyer with a specialty in school shootings, said.

The suggestion underlying much of the coverage was that improvements in the mental health system could have prevented the violence.

Are Violence and Mental Illness Connected?

When mass shooters strike, speculations about their mental health—sometimes borne out, sometimes not—are never far behind. It seems intuitive that someone who could do something terrible must be, in some sense, insane. But is that actually true? Are gun violence and mental illness really so tightly intertwined?

Jeffrey Swanson, a medical sociologist and professor of psychiatry at Duke University, first became interested in the perceived intersection of violence and mental illness while working at the University of Texas Medical Branch at Galveston in the mid-eighties. It was his first job out of graduate school, and he had been asked to estimate how many people in Texas met the criteria for needing mental health services. As he pored over different data sets, he sensed that there could be some connection between mental health and violence. But he also realized that there was no good statewide data on the connection. "Nobody knew anything about the real connection between violent behavior and psychiatric disorders," he told me. And so he decided to spend his career in pursuit of that link.

In general, we seem to believe that violent behavior is connected to mental illness. And if the behavior is sensationally violent—as in mass shootings—the perpetrator must certainly have been sick. As recently as 2013, almost forty-six percent of respondents to a national survey said that people with mental illness were more dangerous than other people. According to two recent Gallup polls, from 2011 and 2013, more people believe that mass shootings result from a failure of the mental health system than from easy access to guns. Eighty percent of the population believes that mental illness is at least partially to blame for such incidents.

That belief has shaped our politics. The 1968 Gun Control Act prohibited anyone who had ever been committed to a mental hospital or had been "adjudicated as a mental defective" from purchasing firearms. That prohibition was reaffirmed, in 1993, by the Brady Handgun Violence Prevention Act. It has only become more strictly enforced in the intervening years, with the passing of the National Instant Criminal Background Check System Improvement Act, in 2008, as well as by statewide initiatives. In 2013, New York passed the SAFE [Secure Ammunition and Firearms Enforcement] Act, which mandated that mental health professionals file reports on patients "likely to engage in conduct that would result in harm to self or others"; those patients, who now number more than thirty-four thousand, have had their guns seized and have been prevented from buying new ones.

Male, Poor, Drug Abuse

Are those policies based on sound science? To understand that question, one has to start with the complexities of the term "mental illness." The technical definition includes any condition that appears in the *Diagnostic and Statistical Manual of Mental Disorders* [DSM], but the DSM has changed with the culture; until the nineteen-eighties, homosexuality was listed in some form in the manual. Diagnostic criteria, too, may vary from state to state, hospital to hospital, and doctor to doctor. A diagnosis may change over time, too. Someone can be ill and then, later, be given a clean bill of health: mental illness is, in many cases, not a lifelong diagnosis, especially if it is being medicated. Conversely, someone may be ill but never diagnosed. What happens if the act of violence is the first diagnosable act? Any policy based on mental illness would have failed to prevent it.

When Swanson first analyzed the ostensible connection between violence and mental illness, looking at more than ten thousand individuals (both mentally ill and healthy) during the course of one year, he found that serious mental illness alone was a risk factor for violence—from minor incidents, like shoving, to armed assault—in only four percent of cases.

That is, if you took all of the incidents of violence reported among the people in the survey, mental illness alone could explain only four percent of the incidents. When Swanson broke the samples down by demographics, he found that the occurrence of violence was more closely associated with whether someone was male, poor, and abusing either alcohol or drugs—and that those three factors alone could predict violent behavior with or without any sign of mental illness. If someone fit all three of those categories, the likelihood of them committing a violent act was high, even if they weren't also mentally ill. If someone fit none, then mental illness was highly unlikely to be predictive of violence. "That study debunked two myths," Swanson said. "One: people with mental illness are all dangerous. Well, the vast majority are not. And the other myth: that there's no connection at all. There is one. It's quite small, but it's not completely nonexistent." In 2002, Swanson repeated his study over the course of the year, tracking eight hundred people in four states who were being treated for either psychosis or a major mood disorder (the most severe forms of mental illness). The number who committed a violent act that year, he found, was thirteen percent. But the likelihood was dependent on whether they were unemployed, poor, living in disadvantaged communities, using drugs or alcohol, and had suffered from "violent victimization" during a part of their lives. The association was a cumulative one: take away all of these factors and the risk fell to two percent, which is the same risk as found in the general population. Add one, and the risk remained low. Add two, and the risk doubled, at the least. Add three, and the risk of violence rose to thirty percent.

Other people have since taken up Swanson's work. A subsequent study of over a thousand discharged psychiatric inpatients, known as the MacArthur Violence Risk Assessment Study, found that, a year after their release, patients were only more likely than the average person to be violent if they were also abusing alcohol or drugs. Absent substance abuse, they were no more likely to act violently than were a set of randomly selected neighbors. Two years ago, an analysis of the National Epidemiologic Survey on Alcohol and Related Conditions (which contained data on more than thirty-two thousand individuals) found that just under three percent of people suffering from severe mental illness had acted violently in the last year, as compared to just under one percent of the general population. Those who also abused alcohol or drugs were at an elevated, ten percent risk.

Mental Illness Not Predictive of Violence

Internationally, too, these results have held, revealing a steady but low link between mental illness and violence, which often coincides with other factors. The same general pattern also emerges if you work backward from incidents of gun violence. Taking a non-random sample of twenty-seven mass murders that took place between 1958 and 1999, J. Reid Meloy, a psychiatrist at the University of California, San Diego, found that the perpetrators, all of whom were adolescent men, were likely to be loners as well as to abuse drugs or alcohol. Close to half had been bullied in the past, and close to half had a history of violence. Twenty-three percent also had a history of mental illness, but only two of them were exhibiting psychotic symptoms at the time of the violence. When you accounted for the other factors, mental illness added little predictive value. Swanson's own meta-analysis of the existing data, on the links between violence and mental health, which is due out later this year, shows the same basic formula playing out in study after study: Mental health problems do increase the likelihood of violence, but only by a very small amount.

Psychiatrists also have a very hard time predicting which of their patients will go on to commit a violent act. In one study, the University of Pittsburgh psychiatrist Charles Lidz and his colleagues had doctors at a psychiatric emergency department evaluate admitted patients and predict whether or not they would commit violence against others. They found that, over the next six months, fifty-three percent of those patients who doctors predicted would commit a violent act actually did. Thirty-six percent of the patients thought not to be violent in fact went on to commit a violent act. For female patients, the prediction rates were no better than chance. A 2012 meta-analysis of data from close to twenty-five thousand participants, from thirteen countries, led by the Oxford University psychiatrist Seena Fazel, found that the nine assessment tools most commonly used to predict violence—from actuarial ones like the Psychopathy Checklist to clinical judgment tools like the Structured Assessment of Violence Risk in Youth—had only "low to moderate" predictive value.

Mental Illness and Suicide

There is one exception, however, that runs through all of the data: violence against oneself. Mental illness, Swanson has found, increases the risk of gun violence when that violence takes the form of suicide. According to the CDC [Centers for Disease Control and Prevention], between twenty-one and forty-four percent of those who commit suicide had previously exhibited mental health problems—as indicated by a combination of family interviews and evidence of mental health treatment found at the scene, such as psychiatric medications—while between sixteen and thirty-three percent had a history of psychiatric treatment. As Swanson points out, many studies have shown an even higher risk of suicide among the mentally ill, up to ten to twenty times higher than the general population for bipolar disorder and depression, and thirteen times higher for schizophrenia-spectrum disorders.

When it comes to the other types of firearms fatalities, though, it seems fairly clear that the link is quite small and far from predictive. After an incident like Sandy Hook [referring to the school shooting at Sandy Hook Elementary School in

Newtown, Connecticut, in December 2012] or Virginia Tech [referring to the school shooting on the campus of Virginia Polytechnic Institute and State University in 2007], policy makers often strive to improve gun control for the future—and those efforts often focus on mental health and the reporting of prior records, as in the case of Connecticut. But if you look at people like Jaylen Fryberg, Mason Campbell [a January 2014 middle school shooter], or Karl Pierson [an eighteen-year-old 2014 school shooter], you see no formal diagnosis of mental illness, and often, no actual signs of instability, either. Even when there are signs, as in Pierson's case, they often remain undiagnosed: Pierson was sent home from a mental health evaluation with a clean bill of health. We'll never know whether counseling could have helped Fryberg. Perhaps it could have. But policy makers should also be focusing on other metrics that may have far more to do with such events than mental illness ever has.

Past Violence Predicts Violence

In all of his work, Swanson has found one recurring factor: Past violence remains the single biggest predictor of future violence. "Any history of violent behavior is a much stronger predictor of future violence than mental health diagnosis," he told me. If Swanson had his way, gun prohibitions wouldn't be based on mental health, but on records of violent behavior—not just felonies, but also including minor disputes. "There are lots of people out there carrying guns around who have high levels of trait anger—the type who smash and break things," he said. "I believe they shouldn't have guns. That's what's behind the idea of restricting firearms with people with misdemeanor violent-crime convictions or temporary domestic-violence restraining orders, or even multiple DUIs [citations for driving under the influence]."

"We need to get upstream and try to prevent the unpredicted: how to have healthier, less violent communities in the first place," Swanson said. Mental illness is easy to blame, easy to pinpoint, and easy to legislate against in regard to gun ownership. But that doesn't mean that it is the right place to start in an attempt to curtail violence. The factors responsible for mass violence are messy, complex, and dynamic—and that is a far harder sell to legislators and voters alike. As Swanson put it, "People with mental illness are still people, and people aren't all one thing or another."

"Being involved in bullying in any way—as a person who bullies, a person who is bullied, or a person who both bullies and is bullied (bully-victim)—is ONE of several important risk factors that appears to increase the risk of suicide among youth."

School Bullying Is Related to Mental Illness and Suicide

National Center for Injury Prevention and Control

The National Center for Injury Prevention and Control is part of the Centers for Disease Control and Prevention, the national public health institute of the United States. In the following viewpoint, the National Center for Injury Prevention and Control explains that bullying does not directly cause suicide. However, bullying can create emotional distress and is one factor among many that can be related to depression or suicidal thoughts. Thus, bullying is a risk factor—for both the bullying victim and the bully—though not necessarily a cause of suicide.

National Center for Injury Prevention and Control, "The Relationship Between Bullying and Suicide: What We Know and What It Means for Schools," April 2014. www.cdc.gov.

As you read, consider the following questions:

1. What does the viewpoint list as three suicide-related behaviors?

2. How are suicide and bullying similar to drowning deaths and parental supervision, according to the viewpoint?

3. What circumstances does the viewpoint say can affect a person's vulnerability to suicide and/or bullying?

In the past decade, headlines reporting the tragic stories of a young person's suicide death linked in some way to bullying (physical, verbal, or online) have become regrettably common. There is so much pain and suffering associated with each of these events, affecting individuals, families, communities and our society as a whole and resulting in an increasing national outcry to "do something" about the problem of bullying and suicide.

For this reason, the Centers for Disease Control and Prevention (CDC) and other violence prevention partners and researchers have invested in learning more about the relationship between these two serious public health problems with the goal of using this knowledge to save lives and prevent future bullying.

As school administrators, teachers, and school staff in daily contact with young people, you are uniquely affected by these events and feel enormous pressure to help prevent them in the future. The purpose of this [viewpoint] is to provide concrete, action-oriented information based on the latest science to help you improve your schools' understanding of and ability to prevent and respond to the problem of bullying and suicide-related behavior.

What We Know About Bullying

- Bullying is unwanted, aggressive behavior among school-aged children that involves a real or perceived power imbalance. The behavior is repeated, or has the potential to be repeated, over time. Bullying includes actions such as making threats, spreading rumors, attacking someone physically or verbally, and excluding someone from a group on purpose. Bullying can occur in person or through technology.

- Bullying has serious and lasting negative effects on the mental health and overall well-being of youth involved in bullying in *any* way including: those who bully others, youth who are bullied, as well as those youth who both bully others and are bullied by others, sometimes referred to as bully-victims.

- Even youth who have *observed but not participated in bullying* behavior report significantly more feelings of helplessness and less sense of connectedness and support from responsible adults (parents/schools) than youth who have not witnessed bullying behavior.

- Negative outcomes of bullying (for youth who bully others, youth who are bullied, and youth who both are bullied and bully others) may include: depression, anxiety, involvement in interpersonal violence or sexual violence, substance abuse, poor social functioning, and poor school performance, including lower grade point averages, [lower] standardized test scores, and poor attendance.

- Youth who report frequently bullying others and youth who report being frequently bullied are at increased risk for suicide-related behavior.

- Youth who report *both* bullying others and being bullied (bully-victims) have the highest risk for suicide-related behavior of any groups that report involvement in bullying.

What We Know About Suicide

- Suicide-related behaviors include the following:

  Suicide: Death caused by self-directed injurious behavior with any intent to die.

  Suicide attempt: A nonfatal self-directed potentially injurious behavior with any intent to die as a result of the behavior. A suicide attempt may or may not result in injury.

  Suicidal ideation: Thinking about, considering, or planning for suicide.

- Suicide-related behavior is complicated and rarely the result of a single source of trauma or stress.

- People who engage in suicide-related behavior often experience overwhelming feelings of helplessness and hopelessness.

- ANY involvement with bullying behavior is one stressor that may significantly contribute to feelings of helplessness and hopelessness that raise the risk of suicide.

- Youth who are at increased risk for suicide-related behavior are dealing with a complex interaction of multiple relationship (peer, family, or romantic), mental health, and school stressors.

What We Know and Don't Know About Bullying *and* Suicide Together

- We know that bullying behavior and suicide-related behavior are closely related. This means youth who report any involvement with bullying behavior are more likely to report high levels of suicide-related behavior than youth who do not report any involvement with bullying behavior.

- We know enough about the relationship between bullying and suicide-related behavior to make evidence-based recommendations to improve prevention efforts.

- We don't know if bullying directly causes suicide-related behavior. We know that most youth who are involved in bullying do NOT engage in suicide-related behavior. It is correct to say that involvement in bullying, along with other risk factors, increases the chance that a young person will engage in suicide-related behaviors.

The Relationship Between Bullying and Suicide

Recent attention focused on the relationship between bullying and suicide is positive and helpful because it:

1. Raises awareness about the serious harm that bullying does to all youth involved in bullying in any way.

2. Highlights the significant risk for our most vulnerable youth (e.g. youth with disabilities, youth with learning differences, LGBTQ [lesbian, gay, bisexual, transgender, and questioning] youth).

3. Encourages conversation about the problem of bullying and suicide and promotes collaboration around prevention locally and nationally.

However, framing the discussion of the issue as bullying being a single, direct cause of suicide is not helpful and is potentially harmful because it could:

1. Perpetuate the false notion that suicide is a natural response to being bullied, which has the dangerous potential to normalize the response and thus create copycat behavior among youth.

What Causes Suicide?

Thomas Joiner's interpersonal theory of suicide (2005) argues that death by suicide requires the interaction of three constructs within an individual: thwarted belongingness, perceived burdensomeness, and acquired capability. The concept of thwarted belongingness can be traced to a theory proposed by [Roy F.] Baumeister and [Mark R.] Leary (1995) arguing that all people share a common need to belong. Joiner's theory posits that the desire for suicide will develop if this fundamental need is not met. This notion builds upon earlier social-psychological conceptualizations in that it isolates the specific interpersonal mechanism at play in suicidal behavior. It also addresses social interaction on a deeper level than merely the presence of relationships, and concerns the nature of those relationships. In other words, a true sense of belonging manifests in the quality of relationships in one's life, not the quantity. . . .

Perceived burdensomeness involves feelings of self-hatred and of being a liability to others. Such feelings of burdensomeness have traditionally been tied to family-related issues such as conflict, illness, and unemployment. However, Joiner expands the reach of this construct to include the relationships that exist outside of the family structure. In other words (and this is arguably relevant to adolescent interactions), feelings of burdensomeness can also be involved in peer interactions.

Christopher D. Corona, David A. Jobes, and Alan L. Berman,
"Social-Psychological Model of Adolescent Suicide,"
Youth Suicide and Bullying: Challenges and Strategies for
Prevention and Intervention. *Ed. Peter Goldblum,*
Dorothy L. Espelage, Joyce Chu, and Bruce Bongar.
New York: Oxford University Press, 2015.

2. Encourage sensationalized reporting and contradicts the "Recommendations for Reporting on Suicide" (http://reportingonsuicide.org), potentially encouraging copycat behavior that could lead to "suicide contagion."

3. Focus the response on blame and punishment, which misdirects the attention from getting the needed support and treatment to those who are bullied as well as those who bully others.

4. Take attention away from other important risk factors for suicidal behavior that need to be addressed (e.g., substance abuse, mental illnesses, problems coping with disease/disability, family dysfunction, etc.).

Still, a report of a young person who takes his/her own life and leaves a note pointing directly to the suffering and pain they have endured because of bullying is shocking and heartbreaking. While a young person's death by suicide is a tragedy and both bullying and suicide-related behavior are serious public health problems, our response to such situations must reflect a balanced understanding of the issues informed by the best available research.

It is particularly important to understand the difference between circumstances being related to an event versus being direct causes or effects of the event. To explore this idea, let's look at a similar but much simpler example.

In the case of drowning deaths among children, those who are not directly supervised by a competent adult while swimming are more likely to die by drowning than those children who are directly supervised. While the lack of adult supervision does not directly cause a child to drown, it is a critical circumstance that can affect the outcome of the situation.

Just as with preventing deaths by drowning, for bullying and suicide prevention, the more we understand about the relationship between circumstances and outcomes the better decisions we can make about what actions to take to prevent bullying and suicide-related behavior.

So, if bullying doesn't directly cause suicide, what do we know about how bullying and suicide are related?

Bullying and suicide-related behavior are both complex public health problems. Circumstances that can affect a person's vulnerability to either or both of these behaviors exist at a variety of levels of influence—individual, family, community, and society. These include:

- emotional distress;

- exposure to violence;

- family conflict;

- relationship problems;

- lack of connectedness to school/sense of supportive school environment;

- alcohol and drug use;

- physical disabilities/learning differences; [and]

- lack of access to resources/support.

If, however, students experience the opposite of some of the circumstances listed above (e.g., family support rather than family conflict; strong school connectedness rather than lack of connectedness), their risk for suicide-related behavior and/or bullying others—even if they experience bullying behavior—might be reduced. These types of circumstances/ situations or behaviors are sometimes referred to as "protective factors."

In reality, most students have a combination of risk and protective factors for bullying behavior and suicide-related behavior. This is one of the reasons that we emphasize that the relationship between the two behaviors and their health outcomes is not simple. The ultimate goal of our prevention efforts is to reduce risk factors and increase protective factors as much as possible.

The bottom line of the most current research findings is that being involved in bullying in any way—as a person who bullies, a person who is bullied, or a person who both bullies and is bullied (bully-victim)—is ONE of several important risk factors that appears to increase the risk of suicide among youth.

> *"Even in specific cases where a teenager or child was bullied and subsequently commits suicide, it's not accurate to imply the bullying was the direct and sole cause behind the suicide."*

Bullying in Schools Does Not Lead to Suicide

Kelly McBride

Kelly McBride is a writer at the Poynter Institute and coeditor of The New Ethics of Journalism: Principles for the 21st Century. *In the following viewpoint, McBride says that there is no evidence that bullying leads directly to suicide. She argues that media outlets often present simple narratives in which bullying or cruelty drives someone to violence. These narratives distort the facts and can be dangerous—by portraying the victim as innocent and heroic, they can contribute to copycat suicide attempts. McBride concludes that journalists need to do better when presenting the complicated facts about bullying and suicide.*

Kelly McBride, "Bullying Is Not on the Rise and It Does Not Lead to Suicide," Poynter, October 25, 2013. www.poynter.org. Copyright © 2013 The Poynter Institute. All rights reserved. Reproduced with permission.

As you read, consider the following questions:

1. How does McBride say bullying is defined?

2. How did Emily Bazelon's reporting complicate the story of Phoebe Prince's suicide?

3. According to McBride, what are three of the most common mistakes in reporting about suicide and bullying?

Every other month or so a story about a child bullied until he or she commits suicide rises into our national consciousness.

Getting the Facts Wrong

This month [October 2013] it's Rebecca Sedwick from Lakeland, Fla.

Before that it was Gabrielle Molina of Queens. And before that it [was] Asher Brown.

All suicides are tragic and complicated. And teen suicides are particularly devastating because as adults we recognize all that lost potential.

Yet, in perpetuating these stories, which are often little more than emotional linkbait, journalists are complicit in a gross oversimplification of a complicated phenomenon. In short, we're getting the facts wrong.

The common narrative goes like this: Mean kids, usually the most popular and powerful, single out and relentlessly bully a socially weaker classmate in a systemic and calculated way, which then drives the victim into a darkness where he or she sees no alternative other than committing suicide. And yet experts—those who study suicide, teen behavior and the dynamics of cyber interactions of teens—all say that the facts are rarely that simple. And by repeating this inaccurate story over and over, journalists are harming the public's ability to understand the dynamics of both bullying and suicide. People commit suicide because of mental illness. It is a treatable problem and preventable outcome. Bullying is defined as an ongoing pattern of intimidation by a child or teenager over others who have less power. Yet when journalists (and law enforcement, talking heads and politicians) imply that teenage suicides are directly caused by bullying, we reinforce a false narrative that has no scientific support. In doing so, we miss opportunities to educate the public about the things we could be doing to reduce both bullying and suicide.

There is no scientific evidence that bullying causes suicide. None at all. Lots of teenagers get bullied (between 1 in 4 and 1 in 3 teenagers report being bullied in real life, fewer report being bullied online). Very few commit suicide. Among the people who commit suicide, researchers have no good data on how many of them have been bullied.

Not a Direct Cause

It is journalistically irresponsible to claim that bullying leads to suicide. Even in specific cases where a teenager or child was bullied and subsequently commits suicide, it's not accurate to imply the bullying was the direct and sole cause behind the suicide.

Reporters are often reacting to other misinformed authorities. For example, Polk County Sheriff Grady Judd explained to reporters that he arrested two girls (one 12, the other 14) in Sedwick's death, after seeing a callous social media post from one of the girls, "We can't leave her out there, who else is she going to torment? Who else is she going to harass? Who is the next person she verbally and mentally abuses and attacks?" While it's a great quote, it implies that this girl has the ability, through random meanness, to inspire others to commit suicide.

"Everything we know about unsafe reporting is being done here—describing the method(s), the simplistic explanation (bullying = suicide), the narrative that bullies are the villains and the girl that died, the victim," Wylie Tene, the public relations manager for the American Foundation for Suicide Prevention, wrote in an e-mail to me. "She (the victim) is almost portrayed as a hero. Her smiling pictures are now juxtaposed with the two girls' mug shots. Her parents are portrayed as doing everything right, and the other girls' parents did everything wrong and are part of the problem. This may be all true, and it also may be more complicated."

Sheriff Judd has a record of grandstanding for the media. Yet, journalists are running with his narrative, despite the fact that experts on bullying and on suicide are suggesting that there has to be more to the story.

What's a journalist to do? Challenge the sheriff. Add more information to place his quotes in the appropriate context.

"Clearly allowing police to make statements about whether a bullying incident was the cause of the suicide is contrary to suicide reporting recommendations. He has no training to make this judgment," said Dan Romer, director of the Adolescent Communication Institute at the Annenberg Public Policy Center at the University of Pennsylvania. "It would have been good if those quotes had been put into context if they felt the need to include them. At this point, the stories are a lot of hearsay. So, it's a shame that the girls are being identified. But this sheriff is clearly on the warpath about this and he can get all the media attention he wants."

Remember the story of Phoebe Prince, a young Irish immigrant attending South Hadley High School near Boston? After she committed suicide in 2009, several of her classmates were charged with a variety of crimes. *Slate* writer Emily Bazelon went back and documented exactly what happened to Prince in the months leading up to her death.

Bazelon described how several of the students were active or complicit in acts of meanness, including veiled references to Prince on Facebook and yelling at Prince from a car. But those acts hardly amounted to the relentless campaign that authorities described when they announced the investigation and charges. Instead, Bazelon's story reveals a girl who was already experiencing mental illness when she arrived at South Hadley and stepped into an intricate and nuanced social reality that includes bad behavior as well as acts of compassion, sometimes by the same kids.

Bazelon has offered a cautionary approach to Sedwick's story as well.

Common Mistakes

When faced with a story about bullying, especially one that involves teenage suicide, reporters can find resources designed to encourage reporting that informs and educates the public. StopBullying.gov recently published media guidelines designed to help journalists include research and resources in their stories that will add important context and avoid common pitfalls. (In 2012, I facilitated several meetings with a group of researchers and experts who advised the government on the creation of these guidelines.)

There are also helpful resources for journalists covering suicide. While there are myriad mistakes that journalists make on these two issues, here are some of the most common ones:

- Perpetuating falsehoods through hyperbole or by confusing anecdotes with facts, such as stating that cyberbullying is on the rise or is an epidemic.

- Implying that suicide is caused by a single factor, like a romantic breakup, a bad test score or being bullied.

- Suggesting, or allowing others to suggest, that bullying is criminal behavior.

- Allowing sources to reach beyond their anecdotal experience. Parents, teachers and school administrators are rarely qualified to describe research or trends.

- Equating all teenage aggression as bullying, when in fact there is a specific definition that involves sustained behavior and a power imbalance.

- Describing an act of suicide in vivid detail so that it creates a contagion effect among vulnerable populations.

- Glorifying a suicide victim in saintly or heroic terms, which could also contribute to the spread of suicides.

- Forgetting to link to local and national resources about suicide and bullying, including warning signs and strategies for intervention.

One reason these stories gain such traction is they are easy to sensationalize and they tap into a common narrative that children today are spinning out of control as a result of technology and popular culture. "It's every parent's worst nightmare," the news stories and opinion pieces tell us.

By contrast, this *Christian Science Monitor* story [Amanda Paulson, "Rebecca Sedwick Suicide: What Response Is Needed to Combat Cyberbullying?," October 15, 2013] seeks out experts and arms readers with research, facts and resources.

Reporters looking for more motivation to steer clear of the popular, yet erroneous narrative need only look at the way this story echoes through history. Whether it's the proliferation of cars, rock 'n' roll music on the radio, video games, cell phones, or social media, we find ways to demonize technology's impact on the young people who embrace it with such enthusiasm. Over time, we look back and marvel at our own hysteria. Bullying and suicide are serious problems. Journalists owe the public more than they are delivering. We owe the public the science and research. We owe the public the knowable facts. We owe the public the nuanced context of individual cases.

Anything less contributes to a misinformed society, which robs communities of the ability to bring about meaningful change.

> "Parents who refuse to vaccinate their children create weak links in the public health system. They directly contribute to the resurgence of communicable diseases, put others at risk and cost us all money."

The *Register*'s Editorial: Change Vaccine Law, End Religious Exemption

Des Moines Register

The Des Moines Register *is a newspaper located in Des Moines, Iowa. In the following viewpoint, the paper's editorial board says that Iowa law only allows vaccine exemptions for schoolchildren for religious reasons. However, administrative procedures have allowed many parents in Iowa to refuse vaccines for other reasons. The editors argue that unvaccinated children may become infected with diseases such as measles and dangerously increase the chance of an outbreak. Iowa should enforce the strict interpretation of the religious exemption law or ultimately should eliminate religious exemptions altogether, the editors conclude.*

As you read, consider the following questions:

1. What was Iowa's vaccine law before 1977, and what does the *Register* say were the consequences?

2. According to the viewpoint, what does Iowa law say specifically is required for a religious exemption to a vaccine?

3. According to the viewpoint, which states allow exemptions for only medical reasons, not religious ones?

Until 1977, Iowa was one of only a few states that did not require any immunizations for schoolchildren. The state also had the highest per capita incidence of both measles and mumps in the country.

State lawmakers overwhelmingly approved legislation requiring children to be immunized against six diseases before they could attend a school or child care. (Today it is eight diseases.) Former Gov. Robert Ray signed the bill into law.

Flash forward almost 40 years. Measles has made a comeback. The most recent outbreak originated at Disneyland in California. So far more than 120 Americans have been infected, including people in states surrounding Iowa. Some legislatures are making it more difficult for parents to exempt children from required vaccines. Preventable diseases are gaining a foothold because an anti-vaccine movement is encouraging parents not to vaccinate their children. Most people being infected with measles were not immunized, according to the Centers for Disease Control [and Prevention].

There is no link between vaccines and autism. The most dangerous aspect of immunizing a child is the risk of getting in a car accident when you're driving him to the doctor, according to one infectious-disease expert. Some physicians are now refusing to treat patients who are not immunized. These doctors don't even want the kids in their waiting rooms.

Yet some parents continue to ignore science, history and the entire global medical community on this issue. This includes too many parents in Iowa. In the 2013–14 school year about 8,000 Iowa children were granted exemptions from vaccinations, triple the number a decade earlier. Iowa law allows schoolchildren to forgo vaccines for medical or religious reasons.

Our medical exemption recognizes Iowans may have legitimate health reasons for avoiding vaccines. That application must be signed by a health care provider. However, the vast majority of parents cite religious reasons. They are not required to cite a specific religion, explain anything, or visit a doctor. They sign a form saying they have a "sincere religious belief," get it notarized to prove their identity and turn it into the state.

Voilà. Iowa has another unvaccinated child in our midst. These kids attend our public schools, go to movie theaters and board airplanes. They are vulnerable to contracting and spreading dangerous diseases.

What isn't being talked about in this state: Iowa lawmakers did not intend for a religious exemption to be so easy to secure. In fact, the Iowa code clearly states this exemption can be used only by parents or guardians who attest immunization "conflicts with the tenets and practices of a recognized religious denomination of which the applicant is an adherent or a member."

Read that line again. A recognized religion. Conflicts with the tenets and practices. Must adhere to or be a member of the religion.

When this exemption was created in 1977, the *Des Moines Register* reported that the religion must be recognized by the Internal Revenue Service. The director of the state's immunization program at the time said he knew of only two religions—the Christian Science Church and the Netherlands Re-

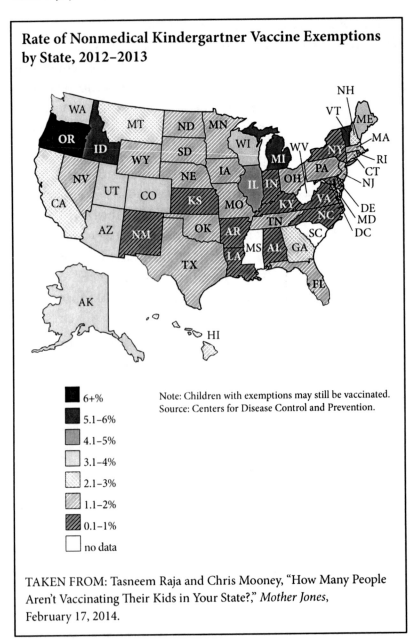

Rate of Nonmedical Kindergartner Vaccine Exemptions by State, 2012–2013

Legend:
- 6+%
- 5.1–6%
- 4.1–5%
- 3.1–4%
- 2.1–3%
- 1.1–2%
- 0.1–1%
- no data

Note: Children with exemptions may still be vaccinated.
Source: Centers for Disease Control and Prevention.

TAKEN FROM: Tasneem Raja and Chris Mooney, "How Many People Aren't Vaccinating Their Kids in Your State?," *Mother Jones*, February 17, 2014.

formed Church—that might qualify. Lawmakers specifically rejected an amendment for a "conscience clause" that would have allowed exemptions for moral or ethical reasons.

For this, the people of Iowa can thank the state's administrative rules, crafted by state workers and boards to implement the law. These rules make no mention of a "recognized" religion that objects to vaccines. Neither does the form filled out by parents. The rules do not reflect the language and intent of the Iowa legislature. The generous interpretation allows parents with no legitimate, religious basis to ignore a law intended to protect public health and safety.

Administrative rules can be changed. Better yet, lawmakers could nix the religious exemption from Iowa code. Mississippi and West Virginia allow exemptions only for medical conditions. A parent's personal, religious, or philosophical beliefs don't matter, and state officials have stood by the strict guidelines. They know vaccines save lives and protect everyone.

Parents who refuse to vaccinate their children create weak links in the public health system. They directly contribute to the resurgence of communicable diseases, put others at risk and cost us all money. When an outbreak occurs, public health workers scramble to track the disease. Schools rifle through student records to send home unvaccinated students.

A 2008 measles outbreak, which started with a 7-year-old boy in California, led to quarantining children and hospitalizing an infant. The net cost of the mess for taxpayers: $10,376 per case, according to researchers.

No one has expressed a religious, personal or philosophical desire to pay the bill.

Vaccine Laws Vary Widely

EXEMPTIONS VARY: Federal agencies regulate, license and recommend vaccines, but there is no federal law requiring schoolchildren be vaccinated. Vaccine requirements and exemptions are crafted at the state level and vary across the country. Almost all states allow religious or other nonmedical exemptions. However, Mississippi and West Virginia allow exemptions only for medical reasons. Last school year, a total of

17 schoolchildren in Mississippi were granted exemptions, compared to about 8,000 in Iowa.

CHANGES: Elected officials in several states are making changes to laws on exemptions, according to the National Conference of State Legislatures. Minnesota lawmakers are considering a bill that would require parents seeking exemptions for personal beliefs to specify and explain each vaccine they're seeking an exemption from and obtain a statement from a physician saying they have discussed the risks and benefits with the parent. Meanwhile, Montana lawmakers are considering adding an exemption for personal beliefs.

HISTORY: Massachusetts was the first state to require immunizations for schoolchildren. It was 1855 and the only vaccine available was for smallpox.

"We need to do what's best for public health and safety, but in a way that avoids doing serious harm to society in the process."

Don't Eliminate Vaccine Exemptions

David Ropeik

David Ropeik is the author of How Risky Is It, Really?: Why Our Fears Don't Always Match the Facts *and a consultant on risk perception and risk communication. In the following viewpoint, Ropeik argues that California's childhood vaccine exemptions should be tightened but not eliminated. Requiring an explanation of why a religious exemption fits the criteria, or asking for an essay about a moral exemption, can quickly reduce exemption rates and allow school populations to reach herd immunity. Eliminating all exemptions, Ropeik says, is unnecessary, violates individual rights, and is an overreaction to a containable problem.*

As you read, consider the following questions:

1. Why does Ropeik say a doctor's note should not be enough for medical exemptions?

2. How does Ropeik suggest economic pressure to vaccinate could be applied?

3. What happened in the early 1900s when smallpox broke out in the United States, according to Ropeik?

The fear of the spread of measles is now swamping the fear of vaccines. Sadly, but predictably, the fear of disease is provoking an overreaction to risk, precisely what the anti-vaccine community is accused of. There are calls in California to completely eliminate personal-belief and religious exemptions for mandatory childhood vaccination. That call, though understandable, is a step too far.

Overreacting to Risk

Yes, opting out of childhood vaccination has allowed nearly eradicated diseases to pop back up. And, yes, this threatens more than just those who decline or delay some or all childhood vaccinations because of environmental values, or libertarian values, religious values, conservative mistrust of government or Big Pharma [the pharmaceutical industry], or just hyper-protectiveness. But the solution need not be to entirely eliminate choice. We just have to reduce the number of people opting out so that enough kids are vaccinated to achieve herd immunity, the level at which enough people are resistant to a disease that it can't spread.

California made opting out harder in 2012—just not hard enough. Raising the bar isn't difficult to envision. For personal-belief exemptions, we might require parents to provide an essay or letter describing their beliefs, and evidence that they apply those beliefs to how they live. For religious beliefs, people should be required to submit a letter from their

priest, rabbi, imam or spiritual leader specifying how their faith precludes vaccination (few do) and evidence that they are living consistently with those religious beliefs. (This is the sort of evidence required in court cases when such conflicts get that far.)

For medical exemptions, a simple note from the doctor isn't enough. There are too many doctors who would either sign a note without any attention (to quickly placate their patient) or who promote non-vaccination or partial vaccination (which, given recommended practice by professional boards, should be challenged as malpractice). Instead, require proof that the doctor has spent 15 to 20 minutes in personal consultation with the parents. One way would be to require evidence of the date and time of the meeting, which can be spot-checked by the local board of health against the doctor's professional schedule.

Economic Incentives

Economic influence should also be applied. People who drive poorly or who smoke, for example, pay more on their insurance to cover the costs of those higher-risk behaviors. States can encourage insurance companies to do the same thing for the higher risk posed by unvaccinated kids. It is entirely justifiable for government to require insurers to do this. Communities pay enormous costs to control outbreaks.

And here's a big one: Personal-belief exemptions based on rejection of solid scientific evidence about vaccine safety should be rejected outright. School systems have to set policy based on what medical experts recommend.

People may disagree with what the evidence says about the minimal risks of vaccines, but school systems are simply not the venue for that fight. Evidence suggests that making it harder to opt out discourages all but the most adamant from doing so. In Florida, Texas and Minnesota, where the administrative burden of opting out is high, fewer parents do so than in Connecticut, Wisconsin and Missouri, where it's easier. And in some states that have recently made it harder, the opt-out rate has dropped. In Washington State, it went down 25% after parents were required to provide a note from doctors saying they'd been educated on the issue.

The evidence shows that it is not necessary to entirely eliminate exemptions to move vaccination rates toward herd immunity levels. Yet that is the extreme action some legislators are calling for. It's what we tend do when we're afraid. We react with emotion first and careful thought second, sometimes at great societal cost to civil liberties.

Americans willingly accepted the [USA] PATRIOT Act [formally, Uniting and Strengthening America by Providing Appropriate Tools Required to Intercept and Obstruct Terrorism Act of 2001, which restricted civil liberties] and unprecedented levels of government surveillance in the fearful days after the 9/11 [September 11, 2001] terrorist attacks. The U.S. sent Japanese Americans to internment camps during World War II. When smallpox broke out in the U.S. in the early 1900s, police in several cities raided homes and clubs and forcibly held people down to be vaccinated. Some were quarantined, others handcuffed and vaccinated at gunpoint. The poor and minorities were especially targeted.

These are fearful times, when . . . a relatively small disease outbreak is getting unprecedented attention, fueling wider public awareness of a serious health threat that has been with us for more than a decade—the undue fear of and resistance to vaccines. But the emotional backlash now threatens to carry us too far the other way. We need to do what's best for public health and safety, but in a way that avoids doing serious harm to society in the process.

Periodical and Internet Sources Bibliography

The following articles have been selected to supplement the diverse views presented in this chapter.

Julie Beck	"Study: Bullied Kids at Risk for Mental Health Problems 40 Years Later," *Atlantic*, April 23, 2014.
Lois Beckett	"What Do We Actually Know About the Relationship Between Mental Illness and Mass Shootings?," *Mother Jones*, June 19, 2014.
Cynthia Canton	"Address Mental Health to Prevent School Violence," *USA Today*, May 9, 2014.
Heather Foster	"Mass Shooters = Mental Illness?," Psych Central, June 29, 2014.
Lauren Fox	"Report: Sandy Hook Shooter Adam Lanza Was Obsessed with Mass Shootings," *U.S. News & World Report*, November 25, 2013.
Caroline Helwick	"Few School Shooters Have Diagnosis of Mental Illness," MedScape, December 5, 2014.
Meghan Hoyer and Steve Reilly	"Low Vaccination Rates at Schools Put Students at Risk," *USA Today*, February 24, 2015.
Phil Plait	"Should Public School Students Get Mandatory Vaccines?," *Slate*, September 24, 2013.
Scott Poland	"Preventing School Shootings: Mental Health Treatment Needed at School," Nova Southeastern University, June 30, 2014.
Jacoba Urist	"How Schools Are Dealing with Anti-Vaccine Parents," *Atlantic*, February 5, 2015.
Romeo Vitelli	"Can Childhood Bullying Lead to Suicide?," *Psychology Today*, September 8, 2014.

For Further Discussion

Chapter 1

1. In his viewpoint, Dewey Cornell of the University of Virginia's Curry School of Education states that from the standpoint of violent crime, students are safer at school than at home. Do you agree? What do you think is the reasoning behind Cornell making this statement? Explain.

2. Kristina Chew discusses a summit of the federal government on bullying and explains that one of the factors hampering efforts to stop bullying in schools is a lack of consensus about what actually constitutes bullying. Why do you think there is not a clear-cut definition of bullying? Do you think that defining bullying in specific terms would help schools reduce or eliminate it? Explain your reasoning.

3. In his viewpoint, Selwyn Duke discusses the Sandy Hook Advisory Commission and its recommendation that certain homeschoolers who are labeled with "emotional, social, or behavioral problems" be closely monitored. Do you think the commission's rationale for this recommendation will help prevent school shootings? Why, or why not? Explain.

Chapter 2

1. After reading the viewpoints in this chapter, do you think better gun policy in the United States will make schools safer? Explain your reasoning, citing text from the viewpoints to support your answer.

2. Kenneth Lovett discusses the New York Secure Ammunition and Firearms Enforcement Act (NY SAFE) gun control policy that expands the state's assault weapons ban.

After reading the viewpoint, do you think the law will be effective in making schools safer in New York State? Why, or why not? Explain.

3. Richard Aborn maintains that teaching children gun safety at home will help reduce the number of school shootings, while Marjorie Sanfilippo argues that teaching children gun safety will not make a difference in the number of shootings. With which author do you agree more, and why? Explain your reasoning.

Chapter 3

1. After reading the viewpoints in this chapter, what security measures do you think can make schools safer? What are some additional measures not mentioned in the chapter that can be taken to make schools safer? Explain why you think these measures would be effective.

2. The use of armed guards in schools seems like it could be a deterrent to school violence, but Nell Gluckman argues that armed guards will not make schools safer. Name at least two positives and two negatives of having armed guards in schools.

3. In his viewpoint, Dan Koller argues against the use of metal detectors in schools, claiming that they create a "cycle of disorder." What do you think Koller means by this? Do you agree with Koller's argument? Why, or why not? Explain.

Chapter 4

1. After reading the viewpoints by Rita Price and Maria Konnikova, do you think there is a link between school shootings and mental illness? Explain your answer, citing evidence from the viewpoints to support your reasoning.

2. The National Center for Injury Prevention and Control explains that youth who report being frequently bullied by

others are at increased risk of suicide-related behaviors and negative mental health outcomes. In light of this, what do you think schools can do to reduce or prevent school bullying? Do you think schools should be the first line of defense in combatting bullying? Explain your reasoning.

3. David Ropeik argues that it is unnecessary to eliminate all childhood vaccine exemptions because community immunity can be achieved if most of the school population is immunized against contagious diseases. Do you think it should be required for all students to be immunized to attend school? What, if any, exemptions do you feel should be respected allowing students to opt out of immunization?

Organizations to Contact

The editors have compiled the following list of organizations concerned with the issues debated in this book. The descriptions are derived from materials provided by the organizations. All have publications or information available for interested readers. The list was compiled on the date of publication of the present volume; the information provided here may change. Be aware that many organizations take several weeks or longer to respond to inquiries, so allow as much time as possible.

American Federation of Teachers (AFT)
555 New Jersey Avenue NW, Washington, DC   20001
(202) 879-4400
website: www.aft.org

An affiliate of the American Federation of Labor and Congress of Industrial Organizations (AFL-CIO), the American Federation of Teachers (AFT) is a trade union that represents more than one million members nationwide, including workers in education, health care, and public service. AFT's mission is to preserve and strengthen a national commitment to reclaiming the promise of American education. AFT's Safe and Welcoming Schools program focuses on combating bullying, reducing class size, and improving school discipline disparities. AFT publishes numerous periodicals, including *PSRP Reporter* and *American Educator*. Its website provides press releases, speeches, position papers, teacher guides, webinars, and articles, such as "AFT, NEA: Arming Educators Won't Keep Schools Safe" and "Create a Safe Environment in Which Bullying Is Unacceptable."

Center for Public Education (CPE)
1680 Duke Street, Alexandria, VA   22314
(703) 838-6722 • fax: (703) 548-5613
e-mail: centerforpubliced@nsba.org
website: www.centerforpubliceducation.org

The Center for Public Education (CPE) is a resource center set up by the National School Boards Association (NSBA). CPE works to provide up-to-date information about public education in an effort to establish more public understanding about America's schools, more community-wide involvement, and better decision making by school leaders on behalf of all students in their classrooms. Among the many articles available at CPE's website are "Search and Seizure, Due Process, and Public Schools" and "The Law and Its Influence on Public School Districts: An Overview."

Community Matters

PO Box 14816, Santa Rosa, CA   95402
(707) 823-6159 • fax: (707) 823-3373
website: http://community-matters.org

Founded in 1996, Community Matters is a nonprofit organization that seeks to collaborate with schools and communities to create safe and inclusive environments where all youth can thrive. Community Matters advocates an "inside-out approach" to making schools safer that focuses on the interpersonal dynamics among the people in the school as the fundamental way to improve school safety and climate. Its Safe School Ambassadors program harnesses the power of students to prevent and stop bullying and violence in schools. Since the ambassadors program started in 2000, nearly seventy thousand students have been equipped with the communication and intervention skills to prevent and stop bullying and improve school climate. The Community Matters website features webinars, articles, and blog posts, as well as information on the organization's many programs and services.

George Lucas Educational Foundation

PO Box 3494, San Rafael, CA   94912-3494
(415) 662-1673
e-mail: info@edutopia.org
website: www.edutopia.org

The goal of the George Lucas Educational Foundation is to improve education through creative, evidence-based strategies that help children become lifelong learners. One way in which the foundation carries out its mission is through the Edutopia website. Edutopia works to spread the word about ideal, interactive learning environments and enable others to adapt these successes locally. Edutopia produces classroom guides and videos, which are available online. The Edutopia blog features articles on school safety, including "5 Ways to Stop Bullying and Move into Action," "Sandy Hook and Hands of Hope: Safer Schools Within Our Reach," and "The Principal Rule: Safety First."

Hoover Institution
434 Galvez Mall, Stanford University
Stanford, CA   94305-6003
(650) 723-1754
website: www.hoover.org

The Hoover Institution at Stanford University is a public policy think tank and research organization. Founded in 1919 by Herbert Hoover, the institution seeks to collect knowledge and generate ideas to secure and safeguard peace, improve the human condition, and limit government intrusion into the lives of individuals. Through publications such as the *Hoover Digest, Defining Ideas*, and *Policy Review*, as well as through research compiled by its task forces and working groups, the Hoover Institution provides information on a broad range of topics, including education. Its website offers position papers, op-eds, videos, blog posts, and articles such as "U.S. Puts Schools on the Hook for Police Actions" and "The Futility of Gun Control."

National Association of School Resource Officers (NASRO)
2020 Valleydale Road, Suite 207A, Hoover, AL   35244
(205) 739-6060 • fax: (205) 536-9255
website: https://nasro.org/

The National Association of School Resource Officers (NASRO) is a not-for-profit organization founded in 1991 with a solid commitment to providing the highest quality training to school-based law enforcement officers to promote safer schools. Made up of law enforcement officers, school administrators, and school security and safety professionals, NASRO has more than three thousand members worldwide. The NASRO website features an "In the Media" section with news clips, podcasts, interviews, testimony, transcripts, and articles such as "School Resource Officer Need Growing After School Shootings" and "Who Should Carry Guns in Schools?"

National Education Association (NEA)

1201 Sixteenth Street NW, Washington, DC   20036-3290
(202) 833-4000 • fax: (202) 822-7974
website: www.nea.org

Founded in 1857, the National Education Association (NEA) is the nation's largest professional employee organization that is committed to advancing the cause of public education. With three million members, the NEA focuses its energy on improving the quality of teaching, increasing student achievement, and making schools safe places to learn. The NEA is engaged in a range of issues that affect public schools, students, and professional school employees, among these issues is school safety. To that end, the NEA has published the "NEA Health Information Network School Crisis Guide" to help school personnel prepare for, react to, and respond to a crisis. The organization's flagship periodical *NEA Today* features articles on school safety, including "Arming Teachers—A Bad Idea That Hasn't Gone Away" and "States Look to Throw Open School Doors to Concealed Weapons."

National Organizations for Youth Safety (NOYS)

901 N. Washington Street, Suite 703, Alexandria, VA   22314
(571) 367-7171
website: http://noys.org

The National Organizations for Youth Safety (NOYS) began in 1994 and is a coalition of national organizations, business leaders, and federal agencies focused on youth engagement and the promotion of health and safety for youth. Its mission is to save lives, prevent injuries, and promote safe and healthy lifestyles among all youth while encouraging youth empowerment and leadership. One of its main areas of focus is violence prevention, including bullying in schools. Its website provides archives of its newsletter, *Notable NOYS Newsletter*.

StopBullying.gov

website: www.stopbullying.gov

StopBullying.gov is a website that provides information from various US government agencies on how teens and others in the community can prevent or stop bullying. Managed by the US Department of Health and Human Services, StopBullying .gov offers news releases, speeches, editorials, fact sheets, and more. The *Stopbullying Blog* offers posts such as "Bullying Gets Under Your Skin: Health Effects of Bullying on Children and Youth" and "Take Action Today: Preventing Bullying from the Very Beginning."

US Department of Education

400 Maryland Avenue SW, Washington, DC 20202
(800) 872-5327
website: www.ed.gov

The US Department of Education is the federal department that establishes federal school funding policies, distributes funds, monitors school performance, and enforces federal law on discrimination. It also distributes financial aid to eligible students and oversees research on America's schools to determine the success of educational programs across the country. The department believes the principal objective of school violence-reduction strategies should be to create climates of safety, respect, and emotional support within educational institutions. There are a range of publications available on the department's website, including handbooks, research papers, speeches, congressional testimony, and in-depth studies on education topics. It also publishes a number of journals and newsletters, including *ED Review* and *Education Research News*.

Bibliography of Books

Nils Böckler, Thorsten Seeger, Peter Sitzer, and Wilhelm Heitmeyer, eds. — *School Shootings: International Research, Case Studies, and Concepts for Prevention.* New York: Springer, 2012.

Dave F. Brown — *Why America's Public Schools Are the Best Place for Kids: Reality vs. Negative Perceptions.* Lanham, MD: Rowman & Littlefield Education, 2012.

Jeffrey W. Cohen and Robert A. Brooks — *Confronting School Bullying: Kids, Culture, and the Making of a Social Problem.* Boulder, CO: Lynne Rienner Publishers, 2014.

Jarrett Conaway, ed. — *Public and School Safety: Risk Assessment, Perceptions and Management Strategies.* New York: Nova Science Publishers, 2014.

E. Scott Dunlap, ed. — *The Comprehensive Handbook of School Safety.* Boca Raton, FL: CRC Press, 2013.

Lawrence Fennelly and Marianna Perry — *The Handbook for School Safety and Security: Best Practices and Procedures.* Waltham, MA: Butterworth-Heinemann, 2014.

James Alan Fox and Harvey Burstein — *Violence and Security on Campus: From Preschool Through College.* Santa Barbara, CA: Praeger, 2010.

Annette Fuentes — *Lockdown High: When the Schoolhouse Becomes a Jailhouse.* New York: Verso, 2011.

Maegan E. Hauserman, ed. — *A Look at School Crime Safety.* New York: Nova Science Publishers, 2010.

Ted Hayes — *If It's Predictable, It's Preventable: More than 2,000 Ways to Improve the Safety and Security in Your School.* Mineral Point, WI: Little Creek Press, 2013.

Lee Hirsch and Cynthia Lowen — *Bully: An Action Plan for Teachers, Parents, and Communities to Combat the Bullying Crisis.* New York: Weinstein Books, 2012.

Shane R. Jimerson, Amanda B. Nickerson, Matthew J. Mayer, and Michael J. Furlong, eds. — *Handbook of School Violence and School Safety: International Research and Practice.* New York: Routledge, 2012.

Judith Kafka — *The History of "Zero Tolerance" in American Public Schooling.* New York: Palgrave Macmillan, 2013.

Jessie Klein — *The Bully Society: School Shootings and the Crisis of Bullying in America's Schools.* New York: New York University Press, 2013.

Paul Langan — *Bullying in Schools: What You Need to Know.* West Berlin, NJ: Townsend Press, 2011.

Peter Langman   *School Shooters: Understanding High School, College, and Adult Perpetrators.* Lanham, MD: Rowman & Littlefield, 2015.

Peter Langman   *Why Kids Kill: Inside the Minds of School Shooters.* New York: Palgrave Macmillan, 2009.

Matthew Lysiak   *Newtown: An American Tragedy.* New York: Gallery, 2013.

David C. May   *School Safety in the United States: A Reasoned Look at the Rhetoric.* Durham, NC: Carolina Academic Press, 2014.

Kathleen Nolan   *Police in the Hallways: Discipline in an Urban High School.* Minneapolis: University of Minnesota Press, 2011.

Brian Schoonover   *Zero Tolerance Discipline Policies: The History, Implementation, and Controversy of Zero Tolerance Policies in Student Codes of Conduct.* Bloomington, IN: iUniverse, 2009.

Marc Thibault   *A Comprehensive School Safety Planning Manual.* Frederick, MD: America Star Books, 2013.

Paul Timm   *School Security: How to Build and Strengthen a School Safety Program.* Waltham, MA: Butterworth-Heinemann, 2014.

| Daniel W. Webster and Jon S. Vernick, eds. | *Reducing Gun Violence in America: Informing Policy with Evidence and Analysis.* Baltimore, MD: Johns Hopkins University Press, 2013. |

Index

R

Racial comparisons
  academic achievement, 55
  bullying and school violence,
    42, 44
  crime victims, 81
  gun ownership, 81
  self-esteem, 55
  use of zero-tolerance policies,
    129–130, 133–134, 144
Raja, Tasneem, 178
*Rampage: The Social Roots of
School Shootings* (Newman), 147
Ray, Brian, 51
Ray, Robert, 176
Recall elections, Colorado, 85,
  86–90
Registries, firearms
  assault weapons, 93
  Germany, 16
  gun rights activists' opposi-
    tion, 68, 104
Religious affiliation, 177–178, 179,
  182–183
Religious exemption, vaccines,
  175, 177–180, 181, 182–183
Resale of guns, 65
Restorative justice practices, 140
Reve, Bjarte, 16
Revolutionary War (1775-1783),
  78
Rigby, K., 43–44
Rocco, Tonette S., 137
Romer, Dan, 172
Romney, Mitt, 87
Ropeik, David, 181–185
Russia, 82

S

Sabato, Larry, 96
Safety drills, 117–118
Safety features, firearms, 69
Saltz, Gail, 126–127, 128
Samuels, Christina, 38–39
Sandy Hook Advisory Commis-
  sion, 50–51
Sandy Hook Promise
  (organization), 60, 62–64, 70–72
Sandy Hook school shootings
  (2012), 92
  gun control initiatives follow-
    ing, 60–64, 66–67, 69–72, 88,
    91–96
  monitoring of homeschoolers
    following, 49, 50–51
  post-event security evalua-
    tions, 123
  same-day attacks, 14
  school security policies fol-
    lowing, 24, 27, 108, 110, 111,
    115
  victims, 50, 61, 63–64, 66, 71,
    72, 74, 99
Sanfilippo, Marjorie, 101–105
Scalia, Antonin, 78
Schneider, Mike, 112
School bus safety, 14–15
School resource officer programs,
  45–46, 139–140
School shootings
  addressing mental illness is
    not good prevention, 151–
    159
  addressing mental illness to
    reduce, 146–150
  denial of epidemic, 24
  gun control can prevent, 60–
    72, 110, 112, 113

CPSIA information can be obtained
at www.ICGtesting.com
Printed in the USA
FFOW05n0257060116

9 780737 775273